# Follow Your Detour

## Let Go of Your Pain, Conquer Your Fear & Find the Real You

Lindsay McKenzie

Copyright © 2019 by Lindsay McKenzie, FYD Creative, LLC

All rights reserved. No part of this publication may be reproduced, distributed, or transmitted in any form or by any means, including photocopying, recording, or other electronic or mechanical methods, without the prior written permission of the publisher, except in the case of brief quotations embodied in critical reviews and certain other noncommercial uses permitted by copyright law.

Although the author and publisher have made every effort to ensure that the information in this book was correct at press time, the author and publisher do not assume and hereby disclaim any liability to any party for any loss, damage, or disruption caused by errors or omissions, whether such errors or omissions result from negligence, accident, or any other cause.

Adherence to all applicable laws and regulations, including international, federal, state, and local governing professional licensing, business practices, advertising, and all other aspects of doing business in the US, Canada, or any other jurisdiction is the sole responsibility of the reader and consumer.

Neither the author nor the publisher assumes any responsibility or liability whatsoever on behalf of the consumer or reader of this material. Any perceived slight of any individual or organization is purely unintentional.

The resources in this book are provided for informational purposes only and should not be used to replace the specialized training and professional judgment of a health care or mental health care professional.

Neither the author nor the publisher can be held responsible for the use of the information provided within this book. Please always consult a trained professional before making any decision regarding treatment of yourself or others.

Some names and identifying details concerning people and places may have been changed to protect the privacy of individuals.

ISBN: 978-1-7338113-4-7

*To Daniel—my everything. Thank you for leading me on this beautiful and adventurous journey and staying by my side every step of the way. Thank you for always believing in me, loving me, and being patient with me. You alone have made all my dreams come true. This is our incredibly beautiful story, and it's perfectly imperfect. I wouldn't change a thing and can't wait to see where our detours continue to lead us. I'll go anywhere with you—I (still) promise!*

*In loving memory of Steve—the best big brother in the world. You inspire me every day to live life to the fullest, love others, and laugh often. I know you're cheering me on from heaven.*

*In their hearts humans plan their course, but the LORD establishes their steps.*

—Proverbs 16:9

# Table of Contents

*Introduction—From Dead End to Detour* .... 1

## Part One: The Dead End
1. No, None, Nothing .... 9
2. Plan B .... 21
3. The Funeral .... 40

## Part Two: The Detour
4. New Attitude .... 55
5. Change of Scenery .... 67
6. Dear Raleigh, It's Not You, It's Me .... 76
7. To Do: Whatever It Takes .... 91

## Part Three: The Journey
8. The Open Road .... 103
9. Learning to Fly .... 122
10. The Destination .... 135
11. The Detour Mindset .... 149

*You're Invited!* .... 167
*Can You Help?* .... 169
*Acknowledgments* .... 171
*About the Author* .... 173

# Introduction—From Dead End to Detour

Normally, hearing "none," "no," or "nothing" is exactly what you'd want to hear from a doctor. For instance, I would have loved it if the doctors had said there was "nothing" wrong with my brother, and "no," he wasn't going to die. Or, when my husband and I supported my mother-in-law through her battle with cancer, it was absolute music to our ears when her doctors informed us that there was "no" more cancer.

But, this time, the doctor's "no" indicated something else: "no," there was *zero chance* of achieving the strongest desire of my heart. There was "no" more reason to continue pursuing my greatest dream. All that I'd ever wanted out of my life: "no," it was not going to happen. It was the end.

Or so I thought.

Let's face it—life rarely goes according to plan. We learn that the hard way, unfortunately. You set out on a path towards your greatest dreams and desires ... only to wind up at a dead end. Everything you've invested—your time, emotions, energy, and sometimes even money—for nothing! Or at least that's what it feels like. Then, you're stuck there, feeling lost and confused with no idea how to proceed. Even if you do recognize a way forward, you can hardly make decisions through the long-lasting pain of the situation and the feeling of brokenness.

But...
What if the dead end is actually your opportunity to take a new route?

What if there's a better path filled with new dreams and desires waiting for you to discover?

What if you've spent so much time "going through the motions" and planning out your life, but those plans aren't in alignment with God's plans for you?

What if He has a greater path, a path you could've never imagined for yourself?

What if He has blessed you with a *detour*?

## You and This Book

This book will support you to find hope in your dead end. It will help you see the world of possibilities that lie ahead of you, even in the darkness of your pain and fear. In reading you'll witness the power of submitting your plans to God and pushing forward in faith. You'll behold the transformational journey that your detour can open to you.

Whether you're facing an unexpected medical condition—your own or another's; a surprising and devastating change in career or financial situation; an unforeseen and heartbreaking relationship upset; a divorce—sudden or not; the loss of a loved one—anticipated or not; a close friend's or family member's betrayal; or some other drastic and difficult change in your life, this book is for you. Let me add too, loss and change don't have to be unexpected to be incredibly challenging and seemingly impossible to navigate. So if you find yourself in a painful place due to a change that you saw a long way off, this book is also for you.

This book will give you the courage to stop sitting around and waiting for answers or just hoping it all goes away. Instead, you'll find inspiration to embrace and follow your detour. This book will give you resolve and spirit to change your perspective. You will learn to equip yourself with a mindset that will give you patience and persistence to keep moving forward, no matter how long it takes to find the purpose in your detour. Your detour stands before you. You simply need help finding it. Let me and this book take your hand.

## Me and This Book

I've experienced loss in a variety of ways—death, infertility, and identity. Some were expected. Some completely blindsided me. And whether foreseen or not, I've been left stunned. Knocked down. Inconsolable. I know the pain firsthand, and, frankly, I'm still in the depths of my very own detour.

I had always imagined my life going a certain way, even from the time I was five-years-old. I had this perfect plan for everything, and I mean *perfect*. From my hair and school work, to my future, I wanted everything to turn out just the way I'd imagined. It didn't come easy either. I worked diligently to ensure my plans materialized. For awhile, things went according to my plan.

Then, one day, those plans came crashing down with the most unexpected and unexplainable news.

What I'd never anticipated, for even a moment, occurred.

More significantly, though, was where that not-according-to-plan new reality—that *detour*—would lead me: to becoming the woman I am today.

As I continue to seek out the meaning in my detour, I've never felt so much purpose, passion, and peace, despite still not having the "answers" I'd hope to have by now.

This book shares the story of how this perfectionist—me—learned to navigate the surprises that life can throw our way. It's a story of losing a lot—my perfect timeline, my hometown, my dream job, my health, and ultimately myself and everything I once believed—in order to gain my true identity and happiness.

## An Invitation and a Promise

I invite you to let me help you find your detour, your new path of personal growth, so you too can uncover purpose, peace, and the real you. You'll discover the beauty in the journey, and you'll learn to slow down and stop rushing towards the destination. I make this bold and big promise too: with this book you will even find a way to be thankful for the dead end you're facing and the pain you're experiencing. Yes, that's my promise to you.

It's time to stop feeling sorry for yourself and wishing things were different. It's time to grieve, but it's also time to let go of the emotions that are holding you back—the fear, anger, disappointment, jealousy, and guilt. You *are* better than that. You *deserve* better, and God *has* better for you. Life is

## INTRODUCTION

precious and short, and you have a promising future waiting for you. Are you ready to become the person you need to be in order to receive it? Are you ready to follow your detour?

Connecting with others has been one of the most valuable aspects of my detour and my greatest motivator for sharing my story. I'd love to hear from you and encourage you along your own detour! Please reach out to me at lindsay@followyourdetour.com at any point as you're reading this book. I'll be anxiously waiting to hear from you! I also invite you to continue following my journey at FollowYourDetour.com.

In the meantime, let's jump into the news that changed everything for me—the story of my dead end.

Part One

# The Dead End

# 1

## No, None, Nothing

*The LORD is close to the brokenhearted and saves those who are crushed in spirit.*

—Psalm 34:18

The doctor opened the door and stepped into the waiting room. As he was scanning the room, our eyes met. His entire face changed, and in that moment, I knew. I knew he was going to share bad news.

Actually, I'd known hours before. He'd said Dan would be out of surgery anywhere from thirty minutes, if they found what they were looking for, to three hours, if they had to look a bit harder. So, after the two-hour mark, my instincts had started to prepare me.

I hardly remember the doctor's words. His mouth was moving, but the entire room was silent. For a second, I blacked out. Everything felt and looked more like a dream. The only words I did hear were "... but Dan is doing well and is in recovery. You can go back and see him here shortly."

I looked over at my two sisters, who'd been waiting with me. I noticed that they were tearing up.

"I'm sorry," the doctor said.

He stood up, patted my shoulder, and walked away.

That's when everything became crystal clear.

It was nothing.

They'd found nothing.

My heart sunk. I started breathing heavily, almost hyperventilating in attempt to hold back the tears.

In a quick second, they were surrounding me, circling me in their arms. My sisters grabbed me, and we sat in silence, crying together and hugging. There was nothing to say. All I wanted to do was be back with my husband.

Normally, hearing "none," "no," or "nothing" is exactly what you want to hear from a doctor. The year before, I would have loved it if the doctors had announced that there was "nothing" wrong with my brother, and "no," he wasn't going to die.

Or, when we supported my mother-in-law through her battle with cancer last year, hearing there was "no" more cancer was absolute music to our ears.

So, what was my husband's medical team looking for?

Sperm—to put it bluntly.

Technically, they were looking for cells that could be harvested into sperm. We had already received the news that Dan had zero sperm in his semen analysis . . . twice. So, the surgery was to go straight to the source (poor Dan!) to find out the cause.

We were so hopeful. "Maybe there's just some blockage," I remember thinking. The doctors seemed hopeful too given Dan's clean medical history and lack of other symptoms (other than elevated hormone levels). As a result, discovering that the surgery was unsuccessful was a huge and devastating surprise.

Let me lighten the mood for a minute and maybe make you laugh, at Dan's expense: when I went back to see him in recovery, I was so nervous about what I was going to tell him. I didn't know if the doctor had informed him of the results or not. As I walked down the hall, I was shaking. My heart was pounding. There was that familiar hospital smell that makes you feel sick to your stomach no matter what you're there for. "Don't cry. Be strong," I kept whispering to myself.

When I got to the recovery area, I paused for a second before I opened the curtain to see him. I took a deep breath and blinked the tears away quickly. I didn't want to show an ounce of disappointment on my face. The most important thing to me in that moment was that Dan was okay.

I opened the curtain and closed it behind me.

Dan immediately informed me, "Well, apparently I'm wearing a diaper," as he held up the sheets and looked under them.

Only *he* could make me laugh at a moment like that, which was *exactly* what I needed. But, that laugh was quickly followed by the question I knew he'd ask, the question that I was dreading.

"You talk to the doctor?"

"Yes," I replied with a shaky little voice and one of those forced smiles that everyone knows is just a cover for bad news.

"What did he say? How'd it go?" he asked with persistence. His eyes anxious.

I shook my head, unable to get words out.

Dan's face dropped. "That's disappointing," he said with an exhale as if he'd been holding his breath.

Dan threw his head back on the pillow and stared up at the ceiling.

My heart broke for him. Up until that moment, it had been *our* problem. But now, it was all on *him*, and I could see the look of defeat on his face. This was no longer about *my* longtime dream of being a mom and us creating new life together. All I could see was a man I love so deeply who just found out that he may never be able to pass on his genes—his "legacy"—as a father. He couldn't give his wife her greatest desire. This whole process, all the pain, it was his "fault."

Little does he know, I fell even more in love with him right there in that hospital bed, diaper and all! I was so grateful that he had even been willing to go through such an invasive procedure for me . . . for *us* and *our* future. I'm sure there aren't many men who would have gone through such measures, and that's just one of the million reasons I love him. He proved to me that day that he would do anything for me.

The lab called the next day to inform us that they'd soaked the tissue sample overnight in some special solution, which can sometimes reveal cells that they couldn't see with the microscope in the operating room. But, even then—nothing. It felt as if they called to tell us our dream was declared officially and unquestionably dead.

## The Final No

The following days got harder and harder. Dan was in incredible physical pain. Both of us were suffering serious emotional pain too. The grief was heavy. It was familiar too since I had just lost my brother one year prior. I remembered feeling the same horrible way the day after I said goodbye to my brother in the hospital. It felt as though my world had come to a complete stop. On the one hand, I didn't know how I was going to move forward, but on the other, I knew, that just like with my brother's death, I'd get through it somehow, some way, with Dan by my side.

Dan, however, was still battling his own personal grief and emotions. "If you want to divorce me, Lindsay, I totally understand" were words I never would've imagined coming out of his mouth. Yet, they were another testament to how much he loved me.

Dan was willing to sacrifice his own happiness in order for me to find mine. This only made me hurt worse because then all I could think was "Why, God, would a man this good not be able to bring life into this world and become the incredible dad he so clearly would be?"

It didn't make sense.

It just wasn't fair.

Dan's doctor called several days later with more news. He informed us that Dan's tissue samples tested positive for Sertoli cell-only syndrome (SCO syndrome). In true Dan fashion, he didn't ask the doctor any questions, so if you're wondering what exactly this means, well, so was I.

As we now understand it, or as Wikipedia puts it, Sertoli cell-only syndrome is a disorder characterized by male sterility **without** sexual abnormality (I'm sure Dan will appreciate me emphasizing the word "without"). It's a condition of the testes in which *only* Sertoli cells line the seminiferous tubules whereas normally, there's sperm cells in between the Sertoli cells as well. What this means is Dan (and any man with SCO syndrome) has no sperm-producing cells. In other words, he's "firing blanks," so to speak.

That's about all the information we have. Other than the fact that it's extremely rare. In fact, when you google it (which I've done at least a million times), the second website that shows up is the Genetic and Rare Diseases Information Center. I think I read somewhere that only about one percent of infertile men are diagnosed with SCO syndrome. So, as I love telling Dan, he *really* is "one in a million." Although we both agree, it would be much better if he were one in a million people who have won the lottery, or something a little more exciting.

There's actually a little more information we quickly obtained through our research on SCO syndrome: it's irreversible, incurable, or whatever word you want to use to express "zero chance," which was all I kept thinking as I scoured the internet. This news felt like the final nail had been hammered into our dream's coffin. Not only did this mean we wouldn't be able to conceive a child *now*, but it meant there was no chance of conceiving in the *future* either

I had to try to find some humor in it. I mean, isn't it ironic that I'd spent so many years avoiding sperm like the plague, and now I was desperate for some! I kept shaking my head and thinking, "All these years we'd been so careful not to get pregnant until we were ready! All these years, I've taken birth control pills for nothing. All those times I freaked out when my period was a day late . . . poor, poor me!" All joking aside though, this diagnosis and it's permanent nature were a tough pill for us to swallow.

So, there you have it. The news that showed me that life rarely goes the way you planned it to go. In fact, life's not fair, and, frankly, sometimes it sucks. At any moment, one thing can happen to you that can totally flip your world upside-down, and—like it or not—those bad things often happen to really good people.

## The Plan

I was so blessed that growing up things typically went as I'd planned. While I had to work hard and it wasn't necessarily easy, life flowed along pretty much in the direction I wanted. I finished high school and got into the college I wanted. I knew exactly what degree I wanted to pursue and finished in four years, just as Dan and I started getting serious. After college, I went on to receive my master's degree and then had several great jobs that helped me land my dream job. Dan and I got engaged, started living together, and had the perfect wedding in Mexico.

We decided on the "five-year plan." Okay, technically this was Dan's choice, but I respected it. We wanted to travel and enjoy our twenties and our marriage for five years before starting a family. By year four, we had purchased our first house. It was fifteen hundred square feet, three bedrooms, had a great backyard, and was in a nice, safe neighborhood—perfect for a family. By the time year five rolled around, we were ready to start having babies. Up until this point, everything had always fallen into place, just the way we wanted it to. So, receiving this news literally felt like our life had come to a screeching halt. The rug had been pulled out underneath us.

I know I'm not the only woman who has enjoyed planning out her life since the time she was little. The game MASH practically ruined us all as little girls. We dream about every little detail in life—our profession, who and when we'll marry, where we'll live, the picket fence around our house, our children's names, etc., etc., etc.

If my life had gone according to my best MASH results, I'd be a teacher, married to Freddie Prinze, Jr., and have four kids (two girls and two boys to be exact). I'd also live in a mansion on the beach in Hawaii and drive a Jeep Wrangler. Luckily, even at nine-years-old, you realize this is pretty far-fetched. I mean, come on, I'd have to fight Buffy the Vampire Slayer to get to Freddie!

But in all seriousness, there was one thing I was absolutely positive I'd achieve in life, if MASH had gone my way or not, and that was having children. It was non-negotiable. Everything else I'd dreamed up for my future was planned around being a mom.

I wanted to get married young, so I could have plenty of time to have as many children as possible. I wanted my children to each be two years apart, so they would be close, like me and my siblings. One of the many reasons I wanted to be a teacher was to have the same schedule as my children when they were in school and to have summers off with them. I planned to stay in Colorado, so my children could grow up near family. I even had their names picked out and had envisioned what they'd look like and the type of mom I'd be to them. I'd thought of *everything* when it came to my future children.

But, it turns out, in the game of "real life," there's no such thing as perfect plans. The saying, "Life is what happens when you're busy making other plans," couldn't be more accurate. There's nothing that can prepare you for that lesson, and in my experience, it's one of the most agonizing lessons in life.

There's no immunity or secret to avoiding the pain of that lesson either. There's also no limit to how much disappointment and suffering you'll face in life due to those unexpected or unplanned events. Oftentimes, it feels like it's piled on you all at once. At least that's how I felt receiving the infertility news just months after losing my only brother.

I wish I could've somehow understood in that moment though that the immense sadness I was feeling was not only temporary, but that it would be an important part of something greater. I wish I'd known then where that news would eventually lead me.

## Your Turn: Dead End to Detour

If you're reading this and you're in the thick of similar pain, then I hope—actually, I'm begging you—stay with me and continue reading. The pain, as much as it hurts, is sometimes necessary for allowing you to take the first step towards a bigger and better path. I know the feeling of having your heart shattered on the floor and having no idea where or how to start picking up the pieces to put it back together.

But, there are *so* many stories out there of people who turned their greatest heartbreak into their greatest blessing. In fact, that's exactly what has happened for me, as you'll see throughout my story. However, I know that's not always helpful to hear when you're in the moment of deep sadness.

Right now, my hope for you is that you can simply acknowledge the pain you're experiencing. First, acknowledge its source because sometimes the source is the result of something good. Ask yourself, "Where is this pain *coming from*?"

For me, the source of the pain of losing my brother was due to the love I had/have for him and the closeness of our relationship. The source of the pain of the infertility news came from the pursuit of a dream, the dream of Dan and me having biological children together. The only way I could have avoided these two times of great pain would have been if I had not loved my brother and our relationship, and if I had no ambition to achieve my longtime dream and desire of having a family with Dan. So, while the pain itself is practically unbearable, its sources are beautiful and honorable.

Pain is sometimes the "price we have to pay" for some of life's greatest treasures during our time here on Earth. Pain can be a result of pursuing faith, hope, and love. Not always, but oftentimes, it's worth it.

So, first acknowledge the source of your pain. Does your pain come from love? Does your pain come from a beautiful dream? Does your pain come from something that was once good? What's the source of your pain?

Next—and this is a big one—acknowledge that this pain may be the catalyst for something greater. You may not believe that's possible, but try to imagine it. Just try.

Maybe your pain is the result of a divorce, for example. Your pain is coming from losing what was once a loving relationship, strong connection, and companionship. Is the present pain worth your once having had those things? Could your pain, therefore, lead you to a new, healthier relationship and a partner better suited for you?

Try to remember that while it hurts right now, someday you'll look back and realize it made you stronger, and it is an important part of your story. Yes, you're going to have to dig deep to do this—but you can do it.

It may take time for you to truly believe there could be purpose in your pain. It will also take time to get back on your feet and feel even the slightest bit of strength in yourself. As you continue to read about my dead end, you'll see how much I stumbled through the process. In fact, the pain continually got worse before it ever got better. In chapter two, I share how I had to be broken down, even more, before I could begin to consider putting the pieces back together.

# 2

## Plan B

*Seek the Lord and His strength; seek His presence continually!*

—1 Chronicles 16:11

Our pain and confusion was all Dan and I could talk about the days and weeks following Dan's procedure. There were a lot of tears and a lot of "What are we going to do?" questioning. We felt defeated, empty, and paralyzed from the heartache.

My obsessive online research continued. I can't even count how many times I googled "Sertoli cell-only syndrome [insert 'treatments,' 'success stories,' 'pregnancies']." I desperately wanted a cure. Then, when I discovered that wasn't possible, I wanted a miracle. I had visions of flying to India for some rare clinical trial that would basically be a magic potion, and—*POOF!*—Dan would have sperm and I would be pregnant.

But, all I could find were a bunch of scholarly articles filled with words I couldn't pronounce. It gave me flashbacks of my least favorite part about college... studying at the library and, coincidently, writing. There were a lot more nos, nones, and nothings: *no* miracle drug, *no* cure, *nothing* that indicated we had any solutions.

I couldn't accept it. Any of it. If one more person told me that we "still have options," I was going to lose it. Sure, they had good intentions and they were trying to help me feel better, but it was only making me feel worse. I hated the thought of any option beyond Dan and I having biological children together. But, based on my research, we felt we didn't have any other choice but to pursue the other "options." It was time to look into plan B.

Ultimately, we wanted a quick fix for the situation. We had invested so much time, money, and energy in all the fertility testing up until this point. We had spent two years and tens of thousands of dollars with nothing to show. We were still empty-handed. How could we just give up? Besides, if you've ever worked with a fertility clinic, then you know how they tend to push you right along. They are, after all, in the business of helping women conceive. They move from one treatment to the next until you're pregnant (and broke!).

Our family and friends would encourage us to "give it time," and in our hearts, we knew we shouldn't rush to a decision. However, we couldn't help but want to reach the "finish line" and have a baby somehow, some way. It was the only way we felt we'd heal from the pain. Then, we could start to forget that any of it had even happened.

Although I didn't like any of the options, I knew that the moment I held our baby, none of it would matter. I kept telling myself to just keep pushing forward. So, we went from talking non-stop about the problem to talking non-stop about the possible solutions: adoption vs. using a sperm donor.

We weighed out the pros and cons, prayed for signs, and changed our minds almost daily. Almost hourly. I had fears and doubts with both options:

- What if we adopt a child and they turn out to be a psychotic serial killer and we're the first victims?
- A sperm donor just sounds icky!
- What if the birth mother changes her mind?
- Would our child someday want to meet their sperm donor?
- What if we never bond with the child we adopt?
- What will people think when we tell them we used a sperm donor?
- What if we want to have more children? What would it be like to have children from different sperm donors or birth parents?

I also talked to anyone who would listen to me about our situation. "What would *you* do?" I'd ask as if that would even help. Of course, I talked with everyone among our families and all of our close friends, but I also talked to so many others as well: my hairstylist, a next door neighbor who I hardly knew, a woman beside me on a plane, my dental hygienist, and even my Uber driver one night.

One of these talks happened to be with my male teaching assistant, which I now realize was probably *very* awkward for him. Turns out, though, he had friends who'd faced a similar situation as us: a young couple who unexpectedly found out they couldn't conceive due to male infertility. They used a sperm donor, were successful, and had a beautiful little two-year-old daughter. My coworker suggested I contact them, knowing they'd love to meet with us and offer their advice.

So, we did. We met at a park and talked for hours as their daughter played. They shared their experience and highly encouraged us to move forward with a donor. They put our fears to rest and assured us that nothing mattered the moment their little girl was born. Strangely, she even looked and acted just like her (nonbiological) dad. Meeting them was extremely comforting and gave us a lot of peace in moving forward.

## Decision Made

The decision was made. We'd do intrauterine insemination (IUI) using donor sperm. We felt that the transition to using donor sperm, instead of adopting, would be quicker and smoother since we had already been working with the fertility clinic. The cost would also be considerably less, and at least I'd have the opportunity to experience being pregnant, something I'd always wanted. Dan felt that a pregnancy would allow him time to bond with the baby in utero, and he was happy that our child could at least have *my* genes. It seemed like using a donor was the closest thing to "normal" that we could get.

I also convinced myself it was probably "normal" that no matter how hard I tried, I couldn't feel very excited about the IUI process. It felt wrong, actually. I had heard of so many women who did whatever it took to get pregnant and have a baby, but I just couldn't look at it that way. I wondered if we were forcing it too much. Were we messing with God's will for us? Maybe I wasn't even meant to be a mom?

I also couldn't help but feel as if I would be doing something *without* Dan. It didn't matter how much he assured me that he would be by my side the whole time and would, without a doubt, embrace the baby as its father. I couldn't bear the thought of getting to look at our baby and say, "She has my eyes!" and Dan never getting to do the same. I just wanted to be on an equal playing field, even if that meant me having to sacrifice ever getting the experience of being pregnant.

Here's the ironic part. I used to always tell Dan, "I hope our kids look exactly like you." I'd always pictured our children looking maybe a touch like me, but most likely him. I'd imagine how much I'd love little mini-versions of Dan, the love of my life, running around. Just the thought of that cuteness was more than my heart could handle! I guess I jinxed myself, but this wasn't the only time I'd done so.

When I was about five-years-old and just learning how to rhyme, I randomly told my mom one day, "I could never marry anyone with the last name 'McKenzie' because then my first name would rhyme with my last name—Lind-*say* McKen-*zie!*" So, I couldn't help but laugh the day I knew I was going to someday marry Dan *McKenzie*, despite his last name. I still laugh sometimes when I hear or write out the name I jinxed myself into.

Needless to say, I'm now *much* more careful with my words! However, taking Dan's last name, rhyme and all, was the greatest honor and gift. So maybe this new jinx of not having a child the way I had planned could be as well. "Keep telling yourself that, Lindsay," I'd think, unwilling to allow any silver lining in all of this.

Clearly, the decision to move forward with a sperm donor wasn't at all easy. But, I chalked it up to being overly emotional and trusted that if it felt right to Dan, it would eventually feel right to me too. I now see that we'd both been thinking of the other's feelings more than our own. All the fears, doubts, questions, signs, and jinxes aside, I chose to keep going through the motions while waiting for my heart to catch up.

Before we could get started with the insemination (*uhhh*—not my favorite word), we were required to have a counseling session. I remember the counselor telling us that she had three adopted children. She had one of the few positive adoption stories I've ever heard. She got each of her children on the very day they were born. They all still had contact with their birth mothers, and the adoption hadn't negatively impacted their well-being and success throughout their childhood.

However, I'll never forget her telling us, "To be honest, if I were to have the sperm donor option back when I was in your shoes, I would've chosen it over adoption. The adoption process is a very emotionally draining rollercoaster."

"Is she even allowed to say that as a therapist?" I remember thinking. But, in my desperation, I thought maybe her advice was God's way of comforting me in our decision. In other words, I took it as another "sign." First sign: meeting the couple who had the daughter from a sperm donor. Second sign: this counselor who was more or less telling us that we should do it (when I wasn't sure she should be). That's two signs! Yes, I was literally keeping count.

The counselor also coached us through how we would tell our child someday: "A nice man gave us a seed to plant in mommy's tummy, so she could grow a baby and that baby was you!" Too much. Too soon. I felt like I was watching a movie and not actually living my life—it was *that* bizarre.

I'd always held my own opinions about sperm donors. Sperm donors are blessings for women who are single, nearing forty, and want a baby, even if it means they will raise it on their own. Sperm donors are a gift for gay and lesbian couples as well. But for me and Dan? It just didn't seem right. I still couldn't make sense of it, and I definitely couldn't find the "blessing" in it.

However, like Dory from *Finding Nemo*, I kept telling myself, "Just keep swimming, just keep swimming." I pictured holding a baby in my arms, and he or she miraculously looking just like a baby Dan. I knew I would love that baby, no matter where it came from. That was the only thing that kept me going.

Our next steps were to select the donor. Weird. It's still weird as I write it. Where do you even begin to search for the man who you'll take sperm from to have a baby with? I remember walking down the aisles of the grocery store, and every man I passed I would rate whether or not he would be a good donor for my future baby. "Hmmm, maybe—if he were about four inches taller ... That one—no way!" And the very occasional, "Hey, not bad!"

This is the picture I couldn't get out of my head: some Joe Schmo off the street walking into a sperm bank, wearing his dirty sweats with messy hair, doing his thing, bringing the container up to the register, collecting his cash, doing an arm pump, and then going on about his day.

For a minute we considered using Dan's brothers' sperm. In fact, they both sweetly offered it. I was surprised by how many people actually suggested this as an option. I guess it makes sense as Dan's brothers share the same genetic makeup as Dan. It would also be as if our child would have a little piece of Dan in him or her. But, talk about an interesting family dynamic that would create.

This scenario seemed way worse when it came time to explain it to our child. "Uncle Adam is *actually* your dad. Well, he's not, but *technically* ... " Would Adam then view our child as *his*? We quickly shut that option down. I mean, Dan's always gotten his brothers' hand-me-downs, but their sperm? Nah.

## Shopping

So, we hit the catalogs and went shopping! Of course, not before I first researched every little detail about the donor process. I was pleasantly surprised that only about five to ten percent of applicants are even selected, so Joe Schmo in his dirty sweats was likely declined. The selection process is extremely strict, and these men (and their families) practically have to be perfect. There were height requirements, medication and health restrictions, and it seemed like the process was such a lengthy time commitment that it was practically a part-time job for the donors.

Before we started browsing, I asked Dan to make a list of things that he would've liked to pass on to a child. We had already agreed that physically, we would select traits that were similar to Dan's. Therefore, the donor would need to be "tall, dark, and handsome," in Dan's words. Okay, let's not kid ourselves, we wanted someone who was a *tad* taller! Why not add on a few little extras here and there? I did the exercise as well. When we finished, we took turns reading them off, like we were playing Boggle:

- athleticism
- compassion
- intelligence
- a sense of humor
- a deep faith
- an adventurous spirit
- hard-working
- integrity
- tenacity

Sharing our lists with each other led to the classic nature vs. nurture conversation. Are these traits and characteristics something we could teach a child? Or, are they genetic? Does anybody *really* know? We sure don't, but we *did* know we wanted to give our child the best shot. I went into the process hoping I'd find a sperm donor who was as similar to Dan as possible, in every way... but just a wee bit taller.

The task became kind of fun as we started putting filters on our search results. Dan would say things like: "I've always wished I was more like six-foot, so let's bump that up." And then, "Blue eyes wouldn't be so bad, especially with dark hair!" It started feeling a little like I was shopping for a date. "This one's a singer songwriter!" I yelled across the room with excitement! "Our kid could be the next American idol!"

We sifted through the narrowed-down selections separately and decided on a strategy. We would each pick our top three and then make the final choice together. We didn't want to influence the other's opinions. I couldn't believe all the information you can access on these donors. It felt like an invasion of privacy. I could read their family medical history, hear a recording of their voice, read a short essay written by them, view photos, etc. My favorite was the staff's impressions of the donors...

"This donor lights up the room every time he walks into the office. He's polite and always very well dressed. He looks a lot like a young Mel Gibson." Every once in a while, we'd hear each other giggle to ourselves as we were making our selections.

I'd occasionally look up and think, "This is not how I pictured baby making." Sure, we each had a glass of wine and the room was dim. We tried to make the process as least awkward as possible, which was fairly similar to the nights when we were trying to perfectly time it for our best chances (before we knew we had zero chance). There's not a whole lot of romance in that either. But, this was even worse.

My heart just ached. My dream was to carry Dan's baby, not some stranger's. I tried to stay out of my head—and heart—and just get this part over with, so we could move forward with the insemination. *Eww* . . . I still hate that word.

Within about ten minutes, we had both selected our top three contenders. Two of those three were the same! The other two donors received honorable mentions and were eliminated.

We both were set on the same donor out of those two. Guess which one? The singer songwriter! This guy was the whole package. First of all, the staff described him as "tall, dark, and handsome" (that's sign three). In his interview questions, he mentioned how his favorite childhood memories were playing sports with his dad. It didn't matter what time of year or what sport, they would play it together, which was *exactly* how Dan grew up.

The kicker was that he was in graduate school for educational psychology. He even shared a little part of my passions since I was a kindergarten teacher with a master's degree in education. Most importantly, he talked about his faith and his family. He seemed very caring and compassionate. Again, just like Dan.

Mr. Singer Songwriter couldn't have been more perfect. Everything from dogs being his favorite animal, to traveling, to the exact same physical features as Dan . . . just taller. I knew for sure I didn't want to see an adult photo of this man. I didn't want to see him out in public one day and recognize him. We did opt to purchase a childhood photo though. (Yes, I did write "purchase." No extras included in the fertility business!) "What if he has a giant, crooked nose like Owen Wilson?" Dan wondered, insisting we pay the thirteen dollars to access the photo.

I remember clicking "Download" and waiting for the image to appear. I can still hear the sound of my finger clicking the mouse button over and over again, trying to open it (despite what Dan tells me, incessant clicking does indeed make it go faster).

Our eyes were inches from the screen, and we were both leaning in. It was like a curtain doing a big reveal very slowly, from top to bottom, as it took *forever* to load. (It probably only took about ten seconds but who has that kind of patience for technology these days?)

Then, there he was . . .

The cutest little baby-faced seven- or eight-ish-year-old boy in a baseball uniform. He was holding the bat back as if he were about to swing it. "That looks exactly like me!" declared Dan in a tone I had never heard him use before. I watched his face look at the photo, and there was something so sweet about that moment. For the first time I felt a little glimmer of hope and excitement. There it was, sign four.

I snapped a photo of the screen with my phone, and my thumbs had never typed so fast as I texted the photo to my mom and sisters and then Dan's parents. "This is a donor we're interested in." I stared at the screen, waiting for their reactions.

When I saw Dan's mom's pop up, I knew Mr. Singer Songwriter was the winner. "Oh my goodness, I thought that was a picture of Daniel!" she texted back. Everyone responded in a similar encouraging way. It ended up being the easiest decision of the whole process.

The next day I called to place an order of Mr. Singer Songwriter's sperm. Again, not exactly how I had pictured the process of becoming a mom. The lady on the other end of the phone informed me that they were having a special promotion that ended the very same day. A sperm sale, yay! Coincidence or sales technique? Definitely sign five! They also had the exact number of vials left that our doctor recommended we purchase. Sign six.

"Ordered the sperm, babe!" I texted Dan after I got off the phone. What every husband loves to hear from his wife, right?

Then, from that point forward, I felt as though somewhere in one of those vials was our baby. Just frozen in there, waiting to be born, and I needed to rescue him or her. That sounds crazy, I know, but I felt a strange burst of energy towards the process. There was a much clearer path ahead, and I felt like sprinting towards it. Little did I know, though, that fertility procedures are nothing close to a sprint. It's more like crawling ... army crawling ... with one arm.

## Hope—From Nonexistent to Sky-High

Deep down, I still couldn't shake the gut feeling I had. It still didn't feel right. The day of our first procedure, in the car on the way to the clinic, I told Dan, "I just want to get through these three rounds of IUI, even if none of them work. I just want to be able to say that we tried it and then move on. Like checking off a box."

Dan gave me the same look you are probably giving right now, the look of—

*What?*

Trust me, I was just as confused as you are (and Dan was). Why did I not really care if the IUI worked? I didn't even know what "moving on" would look like. It doesn't make sense now, it didn't then, and it may never will. As I've said, the only way I can describe it is that I was "going through the motions." It seemed that the signs were pointing in the IUI direction and nowhere else, so I'd feel foolish not to follow.

Our first IUI procedure went fairly well, minus the big fat negative at the end, but the process was pretty smooth. I had a good ultrasound showing plenty of "good follicles." I received a happy face on my ovulation stick, and they timed the big procedure according to my estimated ovulation day. Come ovulation day, i.e., the day of the big procedure, I had to hold my pee for an hour or so beforehand. It felt like my bladder was going to explode the whole time, but the sperm seemed to "cooperate," or so I was told. They swam right out of that turkey baster, or whatever they use, and raced towards my egg. At least that's what I kept visualizing, based on all those sex-ed videos I was forced to watch in school growing up.

The two-week wait was tough, but I hadn't really allowed my hopes to get too high (as you probably already gathered). I knew the chances of it working the first time were slim and that going into a second round would increase the chances. Besides, I'm not sure my hopes were even present, let alone high.

In some weird way I remember feeling a little relieved I didn't end up getting pregnant from that first round because I felt guilty for saying what I had said to Dan in the car. I'm telling you, my emotions were all over the place. Scattered all over the carpet, and each day I would pick one up and wear it like a hat. I didn't know what I wanted or how I felt from one minute to the next.

When the time came for round two, there was a little more pressure. Each round meant more money, more ovulation sticks, and more time away from work for the appointments. In the back of my head I kept hearing our doctor saying, "Since all of Lindsay's tests are good and indicate no signs of concern, the procedure should be successful within three tries." Not only was my body showing itself very capable of conceiving, the vials we were using were highly concentrated with millions of strong swimmers.

But, round two didn't go so well. We were on our third or fourth nurse, despite being told we would be assigned the same person throughout our entire experience at the clinic. Because we kept getting assigned new nurses, when we'd go in for the procedure, the presiding staff wouldn't know us, so they'd ask Dan if he had brought his "sample." I'd have to tell them we were using a donor, you know—pull the knife out of my and Dan's hearts and experience that pain all over again. As if going in the basement of the clinic and picking up our donor sample and carrying it in a tiny pouch up to the appointment wasn't enough of a reminder of our situation.

The second round also entailed a lot more poking and prodding, and even required my nurse to call in backup for help to get that sperm in there. I now realize it's probably because of how tense and angry I was that every time we walked in that clinic, it felt like starting from scratch. Nobody knew us or seemed to care. It came as no surprise, to me at least, that round two failed as well.

By round three, I needed Ovidrel, a shot injected into my stomach to trigger my ovaries to release an egg. Apparently, having more control over when I ovulated would help time the IUI a bit better. With this, I also needed estrogen pills to help build up the lining of my uterus.

It's important to mention that I was teaching kindergarten at the time. Therefore, I was running into the miniature bathroom in my classroom every morning to pee on sticks or to insert little blue estrogen pills up my you-know-what. I'd often hear a tiny knock on that tiny bathroom door followed by a cute little voice, "Mrs. McKenzie? Are you in there? I need you!"

Because the IUI was timed with my cycle—the meds, the appointments, etc.,—my demanding job added to the complexity. I was rushing to the pharmacy to get my prescriptions on my lunch breaks and having to get a substitute teacher in order to go to my appointments. All while holding it together for my little five-year-old students. It started to really wear me down.

Round three was yet another awkward exchange with a nurse who didn't know me and Dan from Adam. I had to fill her in on our entire infertility journey in five minutes before the procedure. I remember lying on that bed with Dan by my side holding my hand. We would look at each other and say a million things without speaking. We both just prayed that the third time would be a charm.

My mentality changed that month too. There's something about trying so hard to make something happen that makes you want it more. I went from "I'm going through the motions" to "This better work, damnit!"

The amount of emotional and physical energy it was requiring took everything out of me. Now more than ever, I just wanted it to be over. But then, after all we'd been through, the thought of not getting pregnant was almost as painful as what we'd experienced when we first got Dan's diagnosis.

Needless to say, the two-week wait was much harder this third round. I tried my best to stay relaxed and positive, and to take care of myself. In my mind, I had nearly every pregnancy symptom under the moon: fatigue, nausea, headaches, and mood swings. I was willing to bet money that this was it (now that I think of it, it did feel a bit like gambling with how much money we were throwing into this whole process with no guarantees).

I started envisioning how I was going to tell our family and what baby items I would buy first. I would catch myself rubbing my belly and whispering sweet nothings to it.

But, yet again, we got the words: "not pregnant." More no, none, nothing—and all the disappointment and suffering that comes with it.

I remember the wrenching pain of that "no" like it was yesterday. It was pretty unbearable. My heart had finally caught up. My hopes had finally reached an all time high, and everything came crashing down. I fell to the bed, exhausted, drained, empty, numb. There was nothing left in me. I had no energy to even cry, and I definitely didn't have the energy to pray. I knew I needed God desperately though. I knew I had no strength left in me, and I needed Him to carry me through this. This desperation was all too familiar and exactly the way I'd felt the night of my brother's death.

That night all the hope I had left for my brother surviving disappeared. I had nothing left to ask God for. I begged Him to just hold me and comfort me. Because He did then, I knew He would again. I lay there on my bed for awhile. Soon enough I felt His peace. And with His peace, I knew I would be able to get back up and rebuild the pieces of myself and my life, even if only an hour at a time.

## Your Turn: From Dead End to Detour

I cried out to Him, and I hope you will too when you feel utterly broken and numb in your pain. Never stop praying, no matter how many times you get knocked down. It's in our greatest moments of weakness that His love and grace can be revealed to us. He's always there, even when we feel like He's forgotten about us. He is your strength.

So many people told me throughout those hard times, "You're so strong," but I honestly didn't *feel* strong. I felt as if I didn't really have a choice. I guess, technically, I did have a choice. I could lie in bed and cry and never leave and stay in that darkness.

Or, I could feel that pain, acknowledge it, but then call to God and allow His peace and comfort to help me get up and get through it, a little at a time. To me, the choice was clear. It might not be as clear for you, so here's a little tough love . . . Life *has* to go on, whether you like it or not. Cry, scream, be angry, lie there awhile. But then—pick yourself up. Take care of yourself. Don't blame yourself. You're strong, you just may not know it yet.

A good friend once told me shortly after she lost her husband, "You have no idea how strong you are until you have to be," and I couldn't agree more. You can't say or believe you aren't strong enough to get through something if your strength has never been tested. When the test comes—when you reach a (seeming) dead end—you'll surprise yourself by how strong you actually can be.

And on those days that you just can't pick yourself up, God will. He will give you a strength you never knew was possible. Ask Him and let Him show it to you. Warning: it may not come instantly, and it may come in a surprising way. In the next chapter, I'll share the unique experience—God's surprising way—that finally allowed me to let go of the pain, so I could begin to build myself up again

# 3

# The Funeral

*The LORD will hold your hand, and if you stumble, you still won't fall.*

—Psalms 37:24

As much as I would like to say that things started to get better for us, they didn't. I wish I could say we started to find peace, but the truth is, we didn't. The pain actually got worse, which didn't even seem possible. We were angrier and more lost than even before. We felt isolated even more than before too.

Nobody knew what to say to us anymore, which was kind of a relief, actually. I wasn't sure how many more times I could hear the same story about somebody's neighbor's daughter's boss who was told she couldn't have children either but *miraculously* got pregnant.

Dan and I didn't know what to say to each other anymore either. "Well, I got what I asked for, I guess. It's over and it didn't work" was about all I could get out. Yep, I'd jinxed myself . . . again.

We were back to feeling paralyzed and lost. I didn't even know who I was anymore. My prayers turned into yelling at God:

"But what about all those signs?"

"Why would You have led us down this path if it wasn't going to take us anywhere?"

"What more do we need to go through?"

My very favorite Bible verse kept popping into my head and causing me more hurt and confusion. Psalm 37:4: "Delight yourself in the Lord, and He will give you the desires of your heart." I fell in love with this scripture when I was in college, busy planning out my future. I clung to it in full belief that it meant I would be given all the things I desired in life. Like God was a genie who would grant me wishes.

One of the greatest desires of my heart has always been to be a wife and mother. My parents got divorced when I was only two years old. They each remarried, and both new marriages also ended in divorce. Divorce was all around me as a child and even as a young adult. Today, nearly everyone in my family and close circle of friends has been divorced. For many people, this would cause reluctance or fear of commitment. For me, it was the opposite. I clung to the hope that I'd find a relationship that would last forever. A love that could endure and be strengthened through the challenges and seasons of life.

As a child, I also recognized that despite my mom's recurring heartbreaks and failed relationships, there was one thing that remained constant for her: the love she had for her children and the fulfillment she found in being a mom, and a great one, I must add. Everything she did in life was for us four kids. She made being a mother look like the most important job in the world, and I couldn't imagine anything else for myself.

I wanted to be just like my mom and give my children everything she'd given me. I knew I'd be a great mother because I'd learned from the best. Plus, I'd put in years of practice with my dolls and babysitting. I wanted it even more than my dream of being a teacher, a role that would later reveal my natural ability to care for and connect with children, thus reinforcing my biggest dream. My nurturing personality is the core of who I am. Like many women, I feel destined to be a mother.

In all my years of attending church, I've always heard that God places those very desires and dreams in our hearts; therefore, He knows them well. But, God *wasn't* giving me the desire of my heart, despite knowing how desperately I wanted a baby. I felt robbed and suddenly that Psalm I loved so much was falling on deaf ears.

I could no longer be on social media and handle seeing another pregnancy or birth announcement. I walked around the school where I taught and could only see parents who, in my biased opinion, were taking advantage of the fact that they had children. "They have no idea how lucky they are," I'd think to myself, even when I'd see their child throwing a tantrum.

Hearing a pregnant woman complain about her symptoms would completely send me over the edge. "I'd give anything to puke every morning and have swollen ankles!" I'd scream at them in my head. I was ashamed by the ugliness of these thoughts and feelings, so I'd try my hardest to hide them behind a smile.

During all this, my sister got pregnant with twins! Two—really? I can't have one, but she gets two? My sister-in-law also got pregnant. A few of my closest friends were "lapping us," as I used to call it, and on to their *second* children.

I watched these women's bellies grow, helped to throw them baby showers, and saw the looks in their eyes when they held their precious babies for the first time. It didn't crush only *me* . . . Dan, too, had to listen to everyone say things like, "Oh, he looks just like you!" and "She has your eyes!" which only reminded him of what he'd never be able to experience. Dan and I both were buried in pain as our loved ones experienced the happiest moments of their lives: the birth of their children.

I never held it against any of them and was genuinely happy for them, aside from my pain. Their children now, especially my twin nieces and nephew, are unbelievable blessings in my life. But, I can't deny that the jealousy was hard to handle.

It just didn't seem fair that it was seemingly so easy for every other woman. It was a dark, lonely time. I didn't see the slightest ray of light in sight. I didn't let anyone know how terribly I was hurting because I didn't want them feeling like they had to tiptoe around me. I wanted them to experience their joy and not be worrying about hurting my feelings.

I didn't even want Dan to know the full extent of these emotions. I knew it would kill him, kill him all over again. He'd take the blame, and he didn't deserve the extra burden of that. So, I held it in and kept it to myself.

I thought about joining a women's infertility support group. But for some reason, I didn't feel like I'd belong there either. Since Dan's condition was so rare, I figured there'd be little chance I'd meet someone else who was going through that type of male infertility. I figured such support groups would be primarily filled with women whose bodies were "failing them." I was afraid I wouldn't be accepted because everything seemed fine with me and my body, or so I thought.

Apparently—yet again—we weren't "average." The doctor originally said the IUI would likely work in three tries, but it didn't. Either way, I felt like our situation was so unique, there was no way anyone in any infertility support group would *truly* understand. It's clear now, though, that I was just being my stubborn self and probably would have benefited greatly from a support group.

But, that's how low and alone I felt at the time: I didn't even think I could relate to women who were in the same boat as me. Regardless of their exact reason for infertility, they too were desperate for a baby, exhausted from failed attempt after failed attempt, and utterly heart-broken. Looking back, I wish I wouldn't have carried this burden alone. There's no honor in pretending to be okay.

## Back on the Wagon

It wasn't long, however, that my hope came back to me just like a swinging pendulum. Or wrecking ball.

Although the initial plan was to only do three rounds, the clinic suggested one final try. Come to think of it, it may have been because no one at the clinic even knew how many attempts we'd tried since they hardly knew who we were. But, I didn't care because I, of course, was back on the "sign" bandwagon and had full confidence that *this* was it! I figured I could get through it one more time.

I should also add that they may or may not have agreed to another round because I may or may not have gone a little rogue after the third IUI procedure. In typical, hormonal, desperate-to-be-pregnant-woman fashion, I called the head nurse and expressed my frustrations with how we were being treated. After painfully listening to me sob for a few minutes, she agreed to take on our case herself. Since I had brought attention to us and called in the big guns, I figured maybe this round would be a little easier.

I approached this final round completely differently. I was more mentally prepared for the additional medications and felt a little more confident in how the procedure would go, now that I had "earned" some special treatment at the clinic. I even got acupuncture for the first time, a thoughtful gift from my lovely sister-in-law.

But, when it came time to do the ovulation tests, I never got that smiley face. This had never been the case. The previous times I'd gotten so in tune with my body that I could feel a pressure in my ovaries right before I was about to ovulate. This time I even tested for a couple extra days, but nothing. No, none, nothing. The ultrasound showed that my body wasn't gearing up for ovulation whatsoever.

Therefore, we couldn't even try that final IUI procedure. It's as if my ovaries went on strike, and, well, I couldn't blame them!

So, there we were, four months into plan B and buried in more nos and nothings. We both had already decided that we would reevaluate the sperm donor route if the IUI didn't work. The next steps that the doctor recommended was in vitro fertilization (IVF). This procedure requires an egg (my egg) to be fertilized with sperm (the donor's sperm) outside the body and then inserted at a later stage. And, if there was anything I was sure about, it was that I wasn't ready for that.

We couldn't afford, financially or emotionally, to take that step quite yet. Besides, performing IVF still didn't give us any guarantee that we'd get a baby out of it. At this point, we felt that our time and money might be better spent on adoption.

We were officially at the end of yet another road and, again, staring at yet another roadblock. Still empty-handed. Still lost. Still devastated. My hope pendulum had swung back to the other side, far, far away. Even still, there was something from my acupuncture appointment that kept resonating with me . . .

## Letting Go

Before poking needles all over me, the acupuncturist sat me down in a private, candle-lit room. The room smelled of essential oils and gave me an instant and overwhelming feeling of calmness. She immediately gained my trust, as she put her hand over mine and looked at me with the most compassionate, twinkling eyes.

She was so sincere in her words, and everything she spoke was like music. Her voice was the perfect soft tone. She began by asking me to share about our infertility journey, ensuring first that I was comfortable in doing so. She couldn't have made me feel more at ease, so the words and tears started pouring out.

It felt a lot like a therapy session, and I hadn't known how badly I needed that. I also didn't know if this was normal for acupuncture because I had never done it before. But, it felt so good to release all those emotions that I'd been keeping from Dan, my friends, and family. Then she asked me a question that she'll never know held so much power for me.

"How have you grieved this loss?"

I immediately started trying to process what she was referring to. Was she talking about my brother? Did I even mention I lost my brother? Grieving was what you did when someone died. What 'loss' was she referring to? We didn't have anything to lose . . . It's all been a bunch of 'nothing,' remember?"

I didn't know how to respond to her, so I looked down and sat there quietly for a minute.

She continued, "You and your husband just experienced the death of your greatest dream of having a child together. That's an incredibly tough loss."

I picked my head up in disbelief that I had never even thought of it that way. For my brother, I grieved in a very healthy way. We had closure with his funeral, we received family counseling, we went through a grief class at church, and we learned a variety of coping strategies. I gave myself grace for the emotions that came with his death: confusion, sadness, and even the ugly ones—anger, guilt—and everything in between. And, yes, these were the very same emotions I was experiencing with our infertility.

It was like a lightbulb went off in my head as she shared more of her wisdom. "I know this sounds silly, but perhaps you and your husband should have a funeral for this dream. Release some balloons or bury a box full of certain items, photos or letters you put together."

It didn't sound silly at all. It made total sense to me. I hadn't viewed our situation as a loss or a death, but that's exactly how it deserved to be treated—and how it felt. I lay there for the rest of the appointment with needles all over my body, yet feeling more at peace.

Just the idea of closure and using a word like "death" felt healing. Relating this loss to the loss of my brother also helped. As sad as I still was and always will be that he's no longer with us, I was dealing with that pain, and rather than moving *on*, I was slowly moving *forward*. Which meant I could do the same for this pain too.

Lying on that table, I fell more and more into relaxation to the point where my entire body was limp. For the first time, I felt a load of pressure lifted from me. I let it go. I'd been holding on so tightly to that dream for the longest time. And then, just like that, I let it go.

I hadn't realized that I'd been carrying it with me—that dream of Dan and I having children, biological children—into every IUI appointment. I'd never really let it go. I wasn't able to grasp on to anything else because I first needed to let go. It's the same way when a loved one dies, the hardest part is letting go and saying goodbye. Then, you realize there's still life after them—it's a different life and you have to find a "new normal"—but you go on, somehow, some way.

That acupuncture appointment was exactly what I needed in order to handle the fourth and final round of IUI though it never ended up materializing. Not ovulating meant I didn't have to go through more appointments, more waiting, more disappointment. It was the ultimate way to close that door and say goodbye . . . for now. I needed the time to grieve the death of my dream and hadn't given myself that time in the beginning.

Dan and I decided it was time for a break from it all and resorted to the one thing that always makes us feel better . . . travel. We went to Thailand and ate incredible food, got massages almost daily because of how affordable they were, and had the time of our lives. It didn't even get to me that the elephant I rode while visiting a sanctuary was pregnant!

Most importantly, we lit a Chinese lantern together the last night of that trip. We both held on tight to it as we lifted it up above our heads and looked at each other, our faces glowing. Then, we let go, and as we watched it drift away into the night sky, we had . . . a funeral.

## Your Turn: From Dead End to Detour

Eventually, no matter how hard you make it for yourself, you'll know when it's time to let go. Despite the confusion you might experience with trying to listen to your instincts or look for signs, you'll come to a point when you're ready. You're fully broken, but ready. And in letting go, you open yourself up to healing.

I wish I had advice to give about knowing *how* to make decisions and *when* to take your next steps after experiencing a painful situation. People will often tell you not to rush and make any decisions while you're still grieving. In the same breath, though, they'll ask, "What are you going to do now?" and expect you to move forward. Otherwise, they'll worry about you.

Plus, it's really hard not to rush. You not only want to heal as quickly as possible, but it can sometimes feel like you don't have time to waste. We're constantly surrounded by things telling us that life is so timely: "Your biological clock is ticking," "You're not getting any younger," "Seize the day." Life can feel like a race at times. You look around at other people's lives and panic because you're "falling behind" and need to "catch up."

Just to put this out there—at times, I think Dan and I rushed into the sperm donor option. Other times, I'm grateful that we gave it a shot and can have peace in knowing we tried.

The thing is, I'm not sure there's an answer. You have to make decisions the best you can, whether you choose to look for "signs," trust your gut, or fall flat on your face because you made a bad decision. You just have to do your best.

Pray for guidance and, sometimes, gamble and see what happens. There are very few decisions that can't be undone or fixed in some way. So take the pressure off, don't beat yourself up, and do what you feel is best for you in the moment. As hard as it is to face, there's no quick fix for pain. There's no shortcut or easy way out. You just have to grit your teeth and bear it.

I will say, however, that Dan and I found more peace when we stopped worrying so much about figuring out our next step. After returning from Thailand, I knew without a doubt that I wasn't ready to get back into trying to conceive. So, we didn't. We agreed to be okay doing *nothing* . . . until it felt right. We decided not to decide on anything. (Finally—a positive "nothing"!)

Just know that there's no timeline, and no one should be telling you how fast or slow to take it. The pain is yours, and you can hold on to it for as long as you need. But, eventually, you have to let it go.

You may never be able to embrace joy again if you're too busy clutching tightly on to that pain. Maybe you need to be reminded that it's perfectly okay to not make a decision at all and do nothing until it feels right. Then, when you're ready to move forward, you'll know.

Even if you try to rush into a decision, God will redirect you if it's not the right path. It may lead to more pain and heartache, but sometimes He isn't necessarily saying, "No," He's just saying, "Not yet." It wasn't much longer after Dan and I returned from Thailand that we started taking steps in a different direction. God began guiding our detour, and even though we didn't fully understand, we trusted Him.

Part Two

# The Detour

# 4

## New Attitude

> *Trust in the LORD with all your heart and lean not on your own understanding; and in all your ways submit to Him, and He will make your paths straight.*
>
> —Proverbs 3:5–6

Even after finding some peace in hitting the "pause button," Dan and I continued to talk about our emotions. We always wanted to make sure we were open and honest about our feelings. It was important to know that we were both on the same page and that neither of us was pretending to feel a certain way in fear of upsetting the other person.

"Do you feel any differently today?" we'd often ask each other. Usually we'd talk in the same circle: we would share with each other that we were both still hurting. Still struggling with trying not to worry about our future. Still wondering whether we'd know when it was the right time to try again and which direction to go.

Yet, we'd both end up in the same place of still not being ready. Talks about adoption would occasionally surface. But, the sperm donor route and IUI procedures had left such a bad taste in my mouth, I couldn't even allow the conversation to go there.

However, there was a moment during one of these talks that completely changed the course of our lives.

"This is just a detour, Lindsay," I can still hear Dan say in a surprisingly enthusiastic way.

We were sitting on the couch in what we called our "coffee room." It sounds fancy, but it was basically one of those entryway rooms that no one knows what to do with. We'd sit there on the weekends and drink our coffee and talk, hence the name. We were facing each other with our legs tangled together. I was slouching down, deep in the couch, because usually these talks only left us feeling more discouraged. But, this talk was different.

"You know what I mean?" Dan continued. "This might be a dead end, but maybe this is also our chance to take a different route. It may not be the path we'd planned for ourselves, but it may be better!"

I nodded, only slightly, looking off in another direction. I needed a little more convincing.

"We have to trust that God has a great plan. The door to having children together may have closed, but that could mean another door full of opportunities will open." Dan isn't usually the positive one out of the two of us, so this was definitely something new.

I think this whole time he had been very careful with his words, knowing that having a child was my dream. He didn't want to say anything that would suggest we should stop pursuing that. I can't blame him one bit for that. Now that I was on the other side of the trying-to-get-pregnant phase, I realized how crazy I'd been with it all. As I, myself, couldn't make sense of my vast range of ever-swinging emotions, I couldn't imagine how I came off to others.

## Pura Vida

Talking about our future and our dreams was something we've always loved doing together. We'd always fantasize about where we'd travel to next and reminisce about where we'd already been. In fact, about three years earlier during one of these talks, we made the decision to blow our entire savings fund that we had built up to buy our first home. We booked a two-week trip to Europe, instead.

It was a moment I'll never forget. We were sitting around a fire pit under the stars in the backyard of a little rental house we had in Denver. It was a perfect summer night. The fire lit our faces as we laughed and talked for hours about the time we'd moved to Costa Rica after we'd first gotten married.

We had no idea what we were doing and had never been there before. We hardly had a plan—no jobs, no place to live—but we had each other and we were going to figure it out. I had just finished getting my master's degree in education and was waiting for my first teaching job. Dan quit his job as an insurance salesman. We were babies, twenty-four and twenty-six years old. Our parents must've thought we were crazy. Other than an all-inclusive stay in Mexico, I had never even left the country. Dan, on the other hand, had studied abroad in college and backpacked through South America using his college graduation money.

Before Dan proposed to me, he sat me down in the park of my old elementary school while we were out for a walk. He needed me to promise him something. He needed to know that if we got married, I would adventure with him. That I would go with him and see the world. Terrible, right? Let me explain.

What he really needed me to promise him was that I'd travel, even if that meant moving away and leaving my family, who was (and still is) everything to me. I said yes, but not without crying and crossing my fingers behind my back, like the seven-year-old me that used to sled down the very hill we were sitting on. I honestly wasn't sure I could leave my family and my home.

I'd lived in Colorado my whole life. The farthest I'd gone from home was attending Colorado State University for college, a measly two hours away. Nobody in my family left Colorado. It was as if there were an unspoken rule that you weren't allowed to. Both my parents were born and raised in Colorado. My mom lived in the same house for over thirty years!

"Why would I ever want to leave my family? Colorado is great! We love it here!" I'm not gonna lie, I put up a fight about it. But, I knew he was worth it. If travel and adventure was important to him, I'd have to honor that if I wanted to marry him.

Besides, I thought, maybe he'd grow out of it. I was pretty good at getting my way—at least at that time I thought I was—so I promised him, "I will follow you wherever you take me in this world."

A few months later, he held up his end of the bargain and proposed!

Can you believe that same girl two years later moved to Costa Rica on a whim? In fact, it was my idea! I came home from work one day and told Dan to pick a spot on the map and we could move there.

At that time I was waiting for a teaching position to open up at the school I'd been working at as a teacher's aide. I fell in love with that school and knew without a doubt it was where I should start my dream career as a teacher. There were three teachers retiring the following school year, and my principal assured me that he'd love to give me one of their positions. In the meantime, he suggested I substitute teach in the building.

Substitute teaching would have been fine. But, I figured, if I was going to kill time waiting for the teaching position, I'd rather spend that time in a more exciting way . . . like bartending somewhere tropical. Also, I could give Dan what he always wanted and get the travel bug out of his system. Then we could come back, have a baby, and live my dream life of being a teacher and a mom of at least three . . . or six.

Needless to say, we went for it. We got married that summer, saved up money, quit our jobs, found someone to watch our dog, subleased our rental house, put our belongings in the basement of said rental house, and bought one-way tickets. We later (and by "later," I mean, as we were boarding the plane) found out that you can't have a one-way ticket to Costa Rica. We needed proof of exiting the country ninety days later when the visa would expire. That's a different story, but it shows how clueless we were. We had no business moving to another country.

Costa Rica turned out to be one of the greatest times of our lives. It was the perfect way to start our marriage and laid the foundation for our relationship. The two of us, in a foreign place, depending on one another. If you're picturing us sitting on the beach sipping Mai Tais every day, let me stop you. We ate Ramen noodles nearly every night for dinner because it was all we could afford, despite working six days a week. We didn't have hot water in our apartment and in order to hear the sound on our TV, we'd have to pull the couch up to it and plug in headphones. It was life in the jungle and we wouldn't have changed a thing.

We worked at a restaurant and made friends with the locals we worked with. We still keep in touch with them today. I even volunteered at a school down there! I gained a whole new perspective on teaching and saw how children can learn and be happy, regardless of the supplies, technology, and equipment available to them. We made enough memories to last us a lifetime.

Let me take you back, now, to our backyard in Denver. Back to sitting around the fire pit reminiscing about our Costa Rican days. "This is what life is about . . . experiences and memories!"

Dan declared, and I finally understood where he'd been coming from all that time.

"You're right," I agreed, "When we're old and grey, will we be telling our grandchildren about the houses we owned or about the adventures we had?"

"Let's go to Europe!" we decided. "When we get back, we can save up more money to buy a house." So, on another whim, we booked those tickets days later. I can picture our parents shaking their heads in disbelief, yet again. "How irresponsible!" I'm sure they were thinking.

We never regretted any of those decisions though. Traveling and adventuring became our favorite thing to do together. You know Dan's travel bug that I'd thought would disappear? Turns out—it bit me too . . . hard.

## The Power of a Name

Now let's circle back to that day on the couch in our coffee room. The couch that was in the three-bedroom house that we eventually bought. We were having the "detour" talk. We were sitting in the very place where we used to talk about our travel memories, along with our dreams and desires, including, but also beyond, our dream of starting a family. The things we'd love to do and experience in this world together. In fact, behind this couch where we sat, was what we called our "travel wall." It was filled with photos from our travels all over the world and quotes about adventure, all serving as reminders of the places we'd been and the places we'd hoped to go.

But, sadly, somewhere along the infertility journey, we'd lost that. Those lighthearted moments and conversations spent reminiscing and dreaming were gone. We'd become completely consumed with talking about the infertility. It hit me hard that while experiencing the loss of our dream of having a baby together, we had also lost sight of our other dreams. We'd forgotten about that foundation we'd built in Costa Rica and our zest for travel and adventure that was a huge part of "us."

It was the first time we realized that maybe we were at a dead end with our fertility journey, but we weren't at a dead end in our story. It was as if we had picked our heads up, wiped our eyes, and discovered this was just a minor roadblock and next to it stood a detour sign. So in that moment, we decided that if we wanted to move forward, we would need to follow that detour. Who knows, it might lead to our next crazy adventure!

It was interesting how much that one word stuck with us: "detour." There was so much power in naming our situation. Giving it a name impacted us in a similar way as the Chinese lantern funeral. "Detour"—the name felt like we were giving life to something new, and who doesn't love new things? New is exciting. It represents possibility!

We started using it every chance we could. "We're taking a detour! There've been some bumps in the road and things haven't gone the way we planned. But, we're faithful that this new path will bring us just as much joy," we would tell people when they asked how we were doing. It was our sales pitch for convincing everybody we were going to be okay and they didn't need to feel sorry for us anymore. Everybody including ourselves. Mostly ourselves.

This concept of a detour became sort of fun. It let us dream again, and we started scheming up our next adventures, the places our detour could take us. Our detour went from feeling like plan B, or an inconvenience, to an exciting exploration into our future. We were embracing it and eager to see where it was going to take us.

What's funnier is that our concept of the "detour" stuck with our family too. Before long, everyone was talking about *their* latest detour—a new job, a divorce, selling their home! And they too were aiming to embrace their detours.

## Getting Grateful

Now don't get me wrong—our pain and uncertainty were definitely still there, deep down. For me, it was the way I looked at it that had completely shifted. One day, out of nowhere, I had the thought, "Maybe God is actually protecting us from something." This was huge!

I had spent so much time being angry that God wasn't giving us our dream. But, I never for a second stopped to think that He could have actually been saving us from something else. Something that could have been even more painful. It's like getting pushed across the road by a stranger and being mad and confused when you hit the ground. But a few seconds later, you realize that your scrapes and bruises are much better than getting smashed by that eighteen-wheeler that had been about to plow into you. I know that God has our best intentions in mind and wants to protect us from harm or pain. I also believe that He uses challenging times to teach us important lessons.

What if my body couldn't carry a baby and if we were to have gotten pregnant, we would have lost the baby? Maybe my own life would have been at risk? What if our genes wouldn't have been a good "fit"? Or perhaps, our baby isn't quite ready to enter the world yet and will be so incredibly worth the wait?

Either way, I was reminded that God is always good, even when things are bad. I knew in my heart that He had beautiful plans for us on this detour. It may be the longer route, but I was convinced that it would be more scenic and give us extra time to enjoy each other along the ride.

Before I knew it, I was thanking God for taking such good care of us. Then, the more I thanked Him, the more things I found in my life to be thankful for. I realized that for two years I had been so focused on what I didn't have (a child) that I had completely overlooked everything I did have.

I have a husband who loves me more than I deserve most days. A husband who proved he would do anything for me and wants nothing more than to make me happy for the rest of my life. Not everyone can say that. In fact, I know many people, who have wonderful children, but are still searching for, or never find, the love of their life like I have. To this day, I continue to tell Dan, "If all I get out of life is you, I'll be the luckiest person in the world. If we someday have children, they'll be a bonus!"

I could go on and on and never be able to count all the blessings I have in my life. Sure, I lost my brother way too soon. But, let me tell you, I had the funniest, most caring brother who was one of my best friends and greatest protectors for twenty-eight years. Some people never get to experience a relationship like that with their brother. Others don't have a brother at all. I have a supportive family, a healthy body, food, shelter, safety . . . you get the point.

You know what else I found myself thanking God for? That very first no we received, the one after Dan's surgery. You see, during this time, we also met a coworker of Dan's and his wife for dinner. This couple had spent ten years trying to conceive. Ten years!

Throughout their journey, they'd had several miscarriages, a few failed IVFs, but zero nos. There was nothing that the doctors could find that was wrong with either of their bodies that could be the cause of their infertility. Hearing about their yes inspired me to appreciate our no. At least we had an answer or cause, no matter how deeply it hurt to hear it.

To clarify, I'm not downplaying the pain and the experiences in life that knock you off your feet, like the death of a loved one or of a dream, in my case. However, you also can't downplay the miracles and blessings that are right in front of your face and all around you in every moment of every day.

## Your Turn: From Dead End to Detour

Sometimes in our pain, we forget who we are, or once were. In the midst of the sadness, we lose sight of our other dreams and passions. Once you're able to start letting go of the hurt, you'll slowly start to see a path to healing ahead of you. You'll understand that this isn't a dead end in your story either.

If it's time for you to embrace your own detour, I hope you have the courage to do so. It may not make sense right now. It may not look like the path you've been planning or trying so hard to create. Have trust that someday you'll look back and understand. Someday you'll be thankful for the struggles you're facing right now, believe it or not.

In the meantime, continue to dig deep inside and try to find the beauty or blessing in your dead end and your pain. Your entire outlook can change by shifting your perspective. Give thanks for the hard times, the suffering, and the agony because you don't know what God could be guarding you from. Be grateful that it led you to the opportunity to take a new path because this detour will be full of new beginnings.

"This will all make sense one day," Dan and I kept telling each other (and often still do). We knew there was a greater purpose for everything that we'd gone through. Piece by piece, it started to unfold, as you'll see in the next chapter—and as it will happen for you too.

# 5

## Change of Scenery

*Do not be afraid or discouraged, for the Lord will personally go ahead of you. He will be with you; He will neither fail you nor abandon you.*

—Deuteronomy 31:8

Nineteen inches of it had piled up on our back deck by the time we woke. The storm had finally ended. The snow had slowed down to the point where you could watch a single snowflake float down. It would land on the blanket of white fluff that was covering everything in sight. There was complete silence outside. Everyone in the neighborhood was hiding inside their homes where it was safe and warm.

For many, especially Coloradans, this sounds like a perfectly peaceful Sunday. For us, there wasn't much peace in our house that snowy day. The fireplace crackled with intensity, and my fingers were aggressively hitting the keys on my laptop.

"That's it, I'm gonna start applying for teaching jobs in North Carolina. I'm so sick of this snow!" I muttered to Dan. He was wrapped up in a blanket beside me watching TV.

"Go for it!" he replied with a chuckle, not taking me seriously.

We'd been playing around with the idea of changing up our scenery a bit. Moving to a new part of town, a new city, or perhaps a new state and region of the country. This wasn't the first time we'd gone through this either. In fact, we used to get in arguments about hypothetical moves.

Anytime we'd visit a new city, Dan would suggest, "We should move here!" I'd entertain the idea, and Dan would jump at the opportunity to discuss it. Then, I'd panic because I couldn't bear the thought of leaving my job, my family, my friends—my comfort!

We'd lived in Colorado our whole lives. It didn't seem possible to leave. Traveling and going on trips here and there was one thing, but moving? Still, those conversations would happen often, no matter how many times they ended in me crying.

"Austin is a great city to visit, but would we want to live there?"

"We could try it for a year!"

"A year? What's the point then? You know how hard it is to find teaching jobs? How do you even know if you like a place in only one year? How would we even make friends that quickly?"

Every time, it was a different city, but the same conversation and fears. To our credit, even before we knew we couldn't have kids together, there was always this strange unsettling feeling that we both shared. We'd brush it off, call it "wanderlust," and book a little weekend getaway somewhere to satisfy it. But, time and time again, it would come creeping right back.

I'd try my hardest to ignore it. I actually felt guilty because, all in all, we had such a great life. We had worked so hard for everything too. Off and on between traveling, we'd finally saved for our first house together. We found one that couldn't have been more perfect for us. It was our dream "starter home" in an adorable suburban neighborhood. After missing out on house after house, we were so excited to secure this one. It had everything we wanted, was beautifully remodeled, and was right in our budget.

We had great jobs too. I'd landed my dream teaching job and had been working at it going on five years. My school had become my second home. I had relationships with the families there and a deep connection to the community I taught in.

I was "Mrs. McKenzie," and that was a big, important role in the tiny world of my kindergarten students. It was more than a job, it was my passion and what I felt I was put on this earth to do. It had its challenges, but the rewards were priceless.

Dan had finally found a great company to work for as well. He loved his coworkers and, for the first time, didn't hate going into the office every day. He got to go on a variety of business trips all over the world! He was making great money on top of the learning and experiences he was gaining.

His jiu-jitsu gym was located near his office too, which allowed him to train on his lunch break. Earning a black belt was a lifelong dream of his. After several years of training, he had already worked up to a purple belt!

That wasn't even everything! We both had new cars, nice things, and finally felt "established." After years of living with our parents or in beat-up rental houses, and working odd jobs to get our foot in the door of our careers, we'd finally made it. We both had master's degrees—and some hefty student loan bills as a result—but we were living the so-called American dream. Sure, we couldn't travel as much as we would have liked because of debt and limited time off, but there's always retirement, right?

## Living . . . Wrong?

So, why weren't we happy? Again, we were feeling this even before we started trying to get pregnant. So, by the time we were through the infertility fiasco, these feelings only became stronger. We were sitting in a house we had bought to raise a family in, and it felt empty. In fact, we had built our entire lives centered around the idea of a family, but it was just the two of us.

Our weekends weren't spent the way a normal young, childless couple would spend them. We'd be doing yard work, or if we were feeling crazy, we'd hit up the neighborhood Chili's for dinner. There was no chance we'd go into the city for a night out with friends. Even though our house was only twenty miles from downtown, it would likely take an hour or more with traffic. We were living the typical suburban life minus children. And . . . is that even possible?

We felt out of place, and our lifestyle only heightened the awareness that we couldn't have children. We also still weren't ready for alternative means of having them. It was starting to feel like we were living wrong, if that makes any sense at all.

Our outlook on life and our mindset had changed with our detour, yet everything around us was the same. It wasn't working. We had to stop feeling selfish for wanting more despite all the great things we had.

The more time that passed, the stronger we felt the need for a fresh start. We wanted a new environment to go along with our new detour. However, there was still a lot of lingering sadness surrounding us that was holding us back from embracing our new path.

I walked around my school feeling like everyone would look at me with these soft eyes, and I could hear them thinking, "There's poor, sweet, sad Lindsay." They had supported me through first, my brother's passing, and next, our infertility struggles.

I'd walk around our house and remember areas I'd lain and cried in for hours, missing my brother or hurting from the pain of a negative pregnancy test. In two short years of living in that house, so much had happened. It served as my place of comfort and safety when the world around me felt out of control. But, now, I felt I needed a new home filled with hope for our future and exciting beginnings.

Our families were all experiencing new chapters as well. My mom sold my childhood home. Our siblings were having babies and building new homes for their growing families. Everyone was experiencing transition and their own detours.

## Learning to Wait

But us? We were feeling physically stuck despite our shifting mindset. We couldn't picture ourselves continuing on, living the same way we had been. It made no sense to wait around for life, or this detour, to reveal itself. We were anxious and ready to run towards whatever it was God had up His sleeve for us.

I often read the words, "Wait on the Lord," throughout the Bible. I had always interpreted this form of waiting as I knew it in its standard definition: "wait—stay where one is or delay action until a particular time or until something else happens" (from Oxford Dictionaries).

"Wait," according to scripture and the Hebrew translation has a different meaning: "to hope, to anticipate, and to trust in the Lord." Waiting on the Lord has nothing to do with delaying action and everything to do with renewing and gaining your strength, as Isaiah 40:31 states: "But those who wait on the Lord shall renew their strength; they shall mount up with wings like eagles, they shall run and not be weary, they shall walk and not faint."

Words like "mount up on wings," "run," and "walk," surely don't sound like delaying action and staying where you are. "Waiting" means having faith, patience, humility, obedience, and often endurance in our suffering. It does not mean sitting, wishing, and twiddling your thumbs as you anxiously hope your situation changes.

Delaying action, for us, would've most likely meant that we'd not only be staying in the same spot physically, but emotionally as well. That definitely didn't feel like putting our faith in and "waiting" on the Lord and renewing our strength.

The detour we envisioned was there, ready to lead us down a new path. It wasn't there for us to wait for; it was waiting on us. It was time for us to step out and push forward in faith. So, we decided we were going to embrace the detour as our new route, and, though we didn't know where it was going to take us, we would follow it while we waited on the Lord.

## A New Love

Consequently, the conversation about moving to a new city on that cold, snowy Sunday was different this time. It was similar to how we'd felt when we more or less threw a dart at a map and chose to move to Costa Rica.

We had started hearing a lot about Raleigh, North Carolina. It seemed everywhere we looked and everything we heard had some tie to Raleigh. We used to joke that Raleigh was calling us and would pick up any object nearby—a remote control, a banana, our dog's paw—and pretend we were having a phone conversation with the city.

I decided to take the first step (yes, doing so conveniently allowed me to avoid the dreaded job of shoveling the snow and having to use the heat pad on my back later), and I began applying to any and every school district in and around Raleigh. I kid you not, the very next day I had a principal contacting me to schedule an interview. Two weeks later, we flew out for three interviews, and, well, we figured we should probably visit Raleigh before we decided to move there.

During that trip, based on our initial impressions, we fell in love with Raleigh! I received all three job offers and accepted a position at an incredible school. The decision, before we had even returned home, had been made.

It wasn't long before Dan landed a position with a company he'd previously worked for and was able to negotiate that the position be one hundred percent remote. Bonus: he even got a pay raise! Four weeks after that, we sold our house, packed up our belongings, said our goodbyes, and were headed in a U-Haul to the East Coast.

Many of our loved ones had concerns about us rushing into the decision, in the same way they had with the sperm donor. We heard a lot of "You sure you guys aren't trying to run from your situation?" We knew it appeared that way but couldn't quite explain the stirring in our hearts.

Our friends and families supported us anyway although we figured they were most likely thinking, "It won't last, they'll be back." It didn't matter, though, because we did what I'd thought was impossible: I left my family and my beloved teaching job, and we followed our detour out of Colorado.

## Your Turn: From Dead End to Detour

Life is a wild ride. The moment we feel lost, we want a map with clear directions for every decision and step along the way. But, no map can contain the unexpected detours and unplanned paths through which your journey actually begins. So, don't wait on life to happen to you. Wait on the Lord while you take action with faith.

You might be surprised to see what life actually has waiting for you, and if you don't follow that detour, you may never experience your greatest and most glorious adventure. It's time for you to give yourself permission to make a change. To step out of the darkness, dream again, and go chase after a new fresh start that's full of possibilities.

It might be scary, but the Lord will go with you, and it could be the beginning of a beautiful story of your own. One you never knew was even possible. Go! Run! Chase after it! Follow your detour!

I hope that as you continue to read about our detour, you find excitement for your own.

Little did Dan and I know at the time, but this was only the beginning of what lay ahead of us. Turns out Raleigh was a stepping stone towards a much greater leap of faith. Hold on tight, my friend, because this is where our story begins to take off.

# 6

## Dear Raleigh, It's Not You, It's Me

> *"For I know the plans I have for you," declares the LORD, "plans to prosper you and not to harm you, plans to give you hope and a future."*
>
> —Jeremiah 29:11

We were pretty smitten with Raleigh from day one. It had everything we love in a city—lots of outdoor recreation, a vibrant downtown, good beer, and Southern hospitality. It also had everything we'd always dreamed of in a city—proximity to the ocean, mild winters, and much less traffic than we were used to. We were so excited to explore not only Raleigh and the rest of the state, but the entire East Coast, which we hadn't seen much of.

We only had about a week to get settled before I started my new teaching job at a year-round school.

I was so nervous, feeling like the "new kid." I couldn't have chosen a better school and community. It felt like home immediately with how welcoming everyone was. I was so ready for the new challenge.

Although I had been teaching kindergarten for awhile, I felt like a first-year teacher all over again. I had new curriculum, a different schedule, and every single process was polar opposite than the way we'd done things in Colorado. I was completely in over my head within the first couple weeks. Change is hard, and so is teaching, so the struggle was real. I was working extra-long hours and would come home completely drained.

Dan, however, was working from our apartment and couldn't wait for me to get home. He'd be eager for some company and ready to go out and try a new restaurant or check out a new part of town that we hadn't yet seen. But me, I wanted to be left alone in a dark room, where no one could find me. Needless to say, we were on completely different pages, which made us feel disconnected and homesick.

Every day I went to work, I'd try to stay positive and set healthy boundaries. Yet, no matter how hard I tried, the job started consuming more and more of me. As the new girl, I held it in and kept a smile on my face. As always, I fell in love with my students and their families. But, it was starting to feel like that wasn't enough for me anymore. I felt my passion for teaching starting to slip away.

I have a confession though. I'm a recovering perfectionist. And, if you know anything about teaching, there's no such thing as a perfect teacher. Still, I was gonna try, even if it killed me . . . and it almost did. I wanted to give my students everything. I wanted to be the best.

I would stay awake at night worrying about every single one of those five-year-olds: "Johnny hasn't been acting himself lately, I wonder if everything is okay at home—I'll talk to his mom at drop-off . . . Sally, Joey, and Katie are falling behind on their letters, I'll get to work early tomorrow and create a special center for them."

Every day on my commute to school my head would spin as I went through my never-ending to-do list. Then, I'd replay the day on the way home. I'd dwell on the moments I wished I could've been more present with the kids or whether I'd done enough for them. I'd usually have a headache from not drinking enough water throughout the day. Many days, I'd even have to bring work home with me.

An unfamiliar city, meeting new friends, and a new job . . . it was a lot to take in all at once. Unfortunately, the honeymoon period of moving to a new city didn't last very long. We were living for the weekends when I could turn my teacher brain off (at least for one of the two weekend days), and Dan and I could explore, adventure, and be together.

## Road Trippin'

On my longer breaks, we would go on road trips. Within only four hours of Raleigh, we could be in so many cool places. We saw so much of North Carolina, but also Savannah, Hilton Head, Washington, DC, and more. So much of our travels up until then had been international, so it was exciting to experience America!

I can hardly put into words what these road trips did for me. I had never felt so alive and free. We'd hardly make any plans. We'd just hop in the car and go. We'd stop along the way wherever we wanted. We'd spend the days biking around cities, hiking, and doing everything and anything that made us happy. The best part was that we could bring along our dogs, which had never been a possibility with our travels before. "This is living!" I would say over and over again to Dan.

At the end of each road trip, we'd inevitably head back towards home, and my spirits would be crushed. There was one particular trip to the mountains, where we spent a week in Brevard, North Carolina, that I cried almost the whole way home.

"I don't want to leave. I wish we could stay here as long as we wanted and then hop in the car and go somewhere else."

That same weekend we were walking around Lake Lure, and across the way, we saw an Airstream. I took a picture of it because there was something about it that screamed "Freedom!" It spoke to me.

One of the dreams Dan and I often brought up during our many chats about our future was RVing around the country when we retired. So, on that drive home from the mountains, amidst the dread of returning back to the grind, I threw out a crazy idea. I had no idea how Dan would respond.

"What if we road tripped full-time? What if we went from rental to rental and stayed somewhere for a few weeks before we moved on to the next place? Better yet, what if we RVed?"

Dan gave me this look like I had completely lost it. A look that I knew meant, "That's impossible!"

It did seem impossible. We were nowhere near retirement, so I'd have to quit my job and I had no idea what I'd do for work. What would we do with all our stuff? We knew nothing about RVing. Not to mention, we had just uprooted our entire lives and moved all the way across the country less than six months before. Everyone would think we were crazy.

## Top Secret Research

But for weeks, it was all I could think about. I started doing top secret research on RVing. I came across blogs of people who were doing it—and not retired! "If it's possible for them, couldn't it be possible for us?" I'd think to myself. Then fear would set in, and I'd shut my laptop before Dan could see.

Every morning on the way to work, though, I'd pray harder than I'd ever prayed before. I wasn't happy and could hardly fake it anymore. I hated when friends and family from home would ask how we were liking Raleigh, and I couldn't say with confidence that we were happy there.

I had thought that Raleigh was going to be the answer for that stirring feeling in our hearts. Yet, that stirring only felt louder and stronger. I worried we'd *never* feel satisfied. Maybe we *were* running from our situation, like our friends and family had thought. What was wrong with us?

I kept telling myself things would get better. It was too soon to give up on our life in Raleigh. We loved the city, so maybe I needed to find a different job and it was time for a career change. But, it wasn't even worth thinking about a new job because I had seven more months left in the school year. I just needed to get through those seven months. I had made the commitment, and I was never one to break that.

Deep in my heart, though, I wasn't sure I could make it. Those familiar feelings were back. I was confused, unsure about my next steps, and full of fear and anxiety. I was yearning to find happiness, and it felt like it had been a long time since I was genuinely happy.

Meanwhile, I continued with my top secret RV research. Somewhere between YouTube videos and blog posts, I discovered a podcast called *The RV Entrepreneur*. Listening to it every day during my commute, I heard stories from people who were working from the road. Young couples, like us, doing a variety of jobs and even building businesses while living out their travel dreams.

I came clean to Dan about my RV research addiction and encouraged him to listen to a few episodes. It only took about two before he became convinced he could continue to work his remote job right from an RV without it having an impact on his work. His excitement spiraled into an obsession as well, and every weekend we were going to RV dealerships to get an idea of what it would cost us.

The funny thing is, we were also working with a realtor to buy a house during this time! Shortly after the move, we began house-hunting. We had come out ahead from selling our house back in Colorado and wanted to reinvest our profit. We wanted to buy a fixer-upper in a growing neighborhood of Raleigh.

The city was booming, and we knew it would be the perfect time to take advantage of the market. Plus, we were certain that we wanted to stay in Raleigh for a couple years. Well, at least we had been up until we got on the RV kick.

We were messes. One minute, we'd be putting an offer in on a house, and the next minute we'd be searching Craigslist for used fifth-wheels. We even got to the point where we were under contract on a house. Then, we ended up losing a thousand dollars of earnest money because we got cold feet.

It finally dawned on us that we should use the money from selling our Colorado house to pay off our student loan debt. It was a much smarter choice than accumulating more debt. Plus, paying off our debt would free us up from a lot of financial stress. This would allow me to quit teaching without having another job lined up right away.

With that thought, we made up our minds. We'd keep exploring the RV dream while we made the most of the next seven months until I could quit teaching. We signed a lease at a brand-new apartment complex within walking distance of downtown, so we could enjoy the rest of our time in Raleigh to the fullest. We also broke the news to our realtor over margaritas and tacos—our treat (it was the least we could do!). After that, we made one of our best decisions ... we paid off those student loans!

## Home for the Holidays

I thought I'd start to feel better knowing there was a light at the end of the tunnel. I could look forward to and actually start planning for RV life, instead of secretly researching it. Yet, every day seemed to only get worse, the more I tried to be patient. I couldn't stay focused, despite my seven-month plan.

My health even started to suffer. The daily headaches continued, and I was always sick with whatever was going around the school. But worst of all, my heart wasn't in it anymore. I was falling out of love with teaching, and that hurt more than anything. It broke my heart that I could no longer give my students a hundred percent. Or that this job that was once my dream was becoming a nightmare.

When we went home that Christmas, I was so nervous about sharing with our family our latest plan of full-time RV traveling. They were still getting used to our decision to move across the country. What on earth were they going to say about this new crazy idea? Our conclusion: no one would take us seriously anymore.

Dan and I talked about it for what seemed like the whole twenty-four-hour drive from Raleigh to Colorado Springs. We practiced how we were going to tell the family. But most of all, we talked about how amazing RVing would be. I could taste the freedom, and the thought of hitting the road and turning those weekend road trips into our everyday life made my heart sing. I was down to six months of teaching left. Which was only nineteen weeks, or ninety-four work-days or so. Yes, I was in full countdown mode.

"Why are you waiting until the end of the school year to quit if you've already made up your mind?" Dan asked me.

To be honest, I hadn't even thought about it that way.

"I can't quit mid-year!" I snapped back at him.

"Why?"

"I just can't. I can't do that to my students. I'd be letting so many people down."

Dan pointed out, "Worrying about what people think of you isn't a reason to stick with something you're unhappy doing. You'll be letting your students down if you can't give them the teacher they deserve because you're so checked out."

I knew he was right, but the thought of quitting my job made me ill.

I'm not even joking when I say we talked about this the entire drive, in between listening to the RVing podcast, of course. I cried, a lot. I knew I wanted to chase this new dream of ours, but I was so scared to let go of teaching. Becoming a teacher was my very first dream as a little one. I had invested so much in that dream. From my undergraduate to my master's degree. Plus, a year of being a teacher's aide. While I had only spent seven years working towards becoming a teacher, it felt like I had waited my whole life for it. Not to mention the financial investment! How could I throw it all away?

During that drive, I broke a tooth! That's how hard I'd been clenching my teeth from the stress. I ended up needing a root canal in another tooth when I went to get the broken one fixed. I couldn't help but feel like that was a sign. I know, there I go again with the "signs." But, I couldn't deny that after the stress of my brother's passing, then the infertility, and now this, my body was suffering. I remember feeling as though I wanted to breathe again without all the heaviness on me.

When we made it home, my family saw the disappointment all over my face. No matter how many times I tried to tell them that I was going to tough it out until the end of the school year, they, like Dan, didn't understand what I was "trying to prove." Nobody understood the battle that was going on inside me.

Our families were also hardly surprised by yet another one of our crazy ideas. I guess we had quite the track record already.

"We're moving to Costa Rica!"

"We're taking our down payment money we saved and going to Europe instead!"

"We're moving to Raleigh, North Carolina!"

They'd heard it all, and we were beyond surprising them anymore. "I just want you to be happy," my mom would tell me again and again.

"Me too, Mom, me too."

After many talks with our family over that week, I made up my mind. I was going to go back to school after Christmas break and quit. Well, at least I said I was. I thought for sure I'd chicken out when it actually came time to do it. On the other hand, I couldn't imagine pushing through another six months.

Could I do it? Probably. Was it worth it, knowing I was going to quit anyway? Was it worth struggling through another six months of my life? My answer was no. I was so tired of hurting and felt I had nothing more to lose, so why not try to go after something I could gain?

Plus, my unhappiness was affecting Dan too. We didn't choose to move to Raleigh to be even more unhappy and spend less time together. Somewhere along the way, we had even lost the excitement for following our detour.

## Wing Check

Long before our detour began, every time we'd book a trip somewhere new, Dan and I would joyfully exclaim, "You can't clip our wings!" Ever since our first adventure to Costa Rica, we always wanted to be free to "fly" away to new places. We didn't want anything to hold us back.

We never wanted to lose that energy and excitement for adventuring and exploring the world together. We've never regretted a single one of those decisions to travel. Our adventures enriched our lives in so many ways. Getting out, seeing new places, and expanding our horizons had become the ultimate fuel for our souls.

On our drive back to Raleigh after Christmas, we realized we were holding ourselves back. Were we trying to clip our own wings? We'd been feeling so guilty for wanting more when we had already experienced more than many people do in a lifetime.

It was as if we felt our dreams were too big, and we needed to tone them down a little. Who were we to think we deserved to live in an RV and travel anywhere we wanted while not having to retire or save up a bunch of money to survive on? We actually felt selfish.

Our parents had spent their whole lives working so hard for everything they had provided for us. They had supported us through college and were so proud of our careers, our accomplishments, and the life we were building. Security and stability was what we knew they wanted most for us. Yet, we had come to a point where we realized that wasn't what we wanted most for ourselves.

We didn't want the "norm." Getting out of the suburbs when we moved to Raleigh opened our eyes to how much of our time was being spent doing housework instead of doing things we enjoy. Moving our stuff across the country, we realized how much crap we had collected that we didn't even need or use. Living in an apartment again showed us that we don't actually need fifteen hundred square feet of living space. Getting out of debt made us want to stay out of debt and stop worrying about owning a home and nice cars. Losing my brother when he was only thirty-three taught us that the time to live is now. The pressure we felt to live the way society was telling us to was too much for us.

"What do we have to lose?" we kept asking each other.

The answer was always—nothing. (There's that word again. We were learning that "nothing" could be a good thing too.)

Yet, why were we so afraid?

"We have the rest of our lives to go back to the suburbs and back to our old lifestyle. But, we may never get the chance to do something crazy like full-time RVing ever again."

"Why wait until we're retired? What if we never make it that long? It's better to travel when you're young, when you have the strength and energy. Plus, you're never retired from being a parent or grandparent, you'll never want to leave family then!"

"YOLO!"

## Failure . . . Or Gateway?

We had so many reasons to go for it. But, the fear was all around us. Our greatest fear was what everyone would think of us. We had already broken the news to our family whose opinion we valued most. But, let's be honest, they'd love us no matter what. What about everyone else? What would *they* think about us?

What would the people at my school think when I quit? What about all the people back in Colorado? We'd prove them right in that it would be true—we didn't last in Raleigh! We'd hyped up our move so much. We had a big going-away party and left with a BANG! And now, eight months later, we'd already be bailing? We'd been telling everyone how much we loved Raleigh, and we did! It had nothing to do with Raleigh, and everything to do with us wanting to pursue a different dream. We felt a little like failures, though, despite having made the decision to go after an even bigger dream.

As I reflected on our time in Raleigh, I realized it was nothing close to a failure. We did something we had always wanted to try but for a long time were too fearful to go for it. Raleigh served a greater purpose for us than just a new place to call home.

Without Raleigh, we may have never sold our house at the perfect time to make the money we used to pay off our student loans. Leaving my comfort in Colorado was also what I needed to break away from teaching. Even before changing schools, I was starting to feel stagnant in the career. I couldn't imagine sticking with it for thirty years until retirement. But, I hadn't had a reason to leave or anything to fall back on.

The move to Raleigh was our gateway to dreaming big. It showed us that we could take big moves in our life and make anything a reality. It allowed me to prove myself wrong. All those things I thought I could never do. Maybe I actually could?

Thanks to Raleigh, Dan also landed his remote job that was now going to allow us to hit the road. It would give me time to transition without having a new job right away and stressing about our finances. So, even though we went through a lot of effort to move across the country for only eight months, it was without a doubt worth it. It was, in fact, a huge success in my eyes. Not in the slightest bit a failure. Again, it was all a matter of perspective.

Taking a detour, doesn't mean that your path will be more clear. There will still be uncertainty and possibly even more struggles and disappointments. With the right outlook, though, you'll have the confidence to keep going. You'll find the assurance you need to know you're headed in the right direction, even when that direction changes.

## Your Turn: From Dead End to Detour

The idea of a "detour" brought on a whole new meaning for us as our time in Raleigh was coming to an end. It became clear that life was actually full of detours and you always need to keep your eye out for them and embrace them. Some detours are the result of a dead end, and others are your own choice because you're ready to go in a new direction.

One detour might lead to another detour and even another. The important thing is knowing that you don't have to stay on a path because of what others might be thinking or telling you. The path you're on now might even be a pretty good one, but if you feel your dreams taking you elsewhere, don't ignore that. Don't feel like you have to explain yourself either.

Following your detour often involves walking away from something—a relationship, a job, a city—so you can walk towards something new and greater. You can't let others, or yourself, stand in your way. The best time to go after a life you love is right now. In fact, you'll see how strongly I feel about taking action in the next chapter. I'll share another scary leap of faith I had to take in order to continue following my detour.

# 7

## To Do: Whatever It Takes

*With God all things are possible.*

—Matthew 19:26

We were very intimidated by everything we had to do to make our dream of full-time RVing a reality. It felt like we were staring up at a giant mountain. We started writing everything we needed to do down on paper. Our list had twenty-nine tasks to tackle before we could hit the road. There were likely twenty-nine more things we were forgetting too because we were so clueless. We had no idea what we were getting ourselves into.

The top two items, though, kept jumping off the paper at me. They seemed impossible, and we knew they were going to be the biggest hurdles to overcome:

1. Lindsay quitting her job

2. Figuring out how to get out of the apartment lease we had signed a month ago that bound us for another seven months

## Item 1: Quitting Teaching

I struggle to even find the words to express how terrified I was to leave teaching. It might actually be, to this day, the biggest fear I've had to face (except for skydiving ... wait until you read about that one!). Once again, the fear was coming from worrying about what people were going to think of me.

I started noticing a trend about myself—I have an intense desire to please people. I wanted to appear as trustworthy, honorable, reliable, and every other good word you would use to describe a person that everyone likes and respects. I could recount so many times in my life when I tried to be perfect for other people. I was more concerned about my image rather than being myself and doing what was best for me, as long as it didn't hurt anyone (see, there I go).

For the first time, I felt it was time to choose me. It wasn't easy. At first, I thought I'd lie to everyone at school and say we had to move back to Colorado for some reason. I started brainstorming excuses I could give for quitting rather than owning up to the fact that I was unhappy. I wanted the easy way out.

At that time, Dan and I started listening to motivational audio-books to pass the time in the car on our road trips. One of the books struck a chord with me, as it talked about how much our values impact our decisions in life. When we value things we cannot control, like people's thoughts or reactions to our decisions, we will never find satisfaction. But, if we value what we can control—standing up for ourselves, respecting ourselves, honesty—it's easier to focus on what's more important and make decisions that we can feel satisfied with. So, I knew I needed to do the right thing, in the right way, but knowing is one thing and following through is another.

Have I made it clear yet how scared I was about disappointing my principal, coworkers, students, and their parents? I played out situations and conversations that I was certain would occur. I envisioned my principal getting angry with me for having to find a replacement halfway through the school year. I was certain she would regret hiring me in the first place.

I pictured my coworkers shaking their heads and refusing to talk to me during my final days there. After all, they had helped select me during the interview process. I also knew for a fact I would receive phone calls and letters from parents. They'd be freaking out about switching teachers mid-year and how that would impact their child's first year of elementary school. I'd lie in bed and see the sadness on my students' faces and agonize over who was going to take my place. Would they take good care of "my babies"? How could I trust anyone other than myself to do what was best for them?

That first day back to work, I knew I couldn't wait to talk to my principal. It would eat at me if I didn't let it all out as soon as possible. So, I scheduled some time on her calendar. With knees shaking, heart pounding, and a giant lump in my throat, I walked into her office. The moment I caught her eyes and she gave me that same smile that she'd smiled the first time we met, I sat down and started crying!

"This is so hard for me right now," I managed to say, and she knew.

"I'm not happy," I continued, and then, right there, a sense of calmness took over my body. "I did it," I thought. "It's over. That wasn't so bad."

It actually wasn't bad at all. My principal, being the incredible woman she is and seeing how hard it was for me, couldn't have been more understanding.

"Lindsay, I always say that all you can do is have good intentions. I know you came here with the best of intentions. You served our school and community well, and in my eyes, that's a success. Just because you aren't staying the entire school year, doesn't mean you've failed. It's time for you to take care of yourself," she assured me.

"The school year will continue, and the world will keep spinning. We will find a replacement, and they'll never be as wonderful as you are, but the school year will go on. Your students will be fine. So, don't you worry."

I hope someday she understands how powerful her words were for me during that time in my life. She hugged me and told me, in the same way my former principal in Colorado had told me, "As long as I'm the principal here, you will always have a job, should you wish to come back!"

My students were sad, but they were also five years old, so they snapped back pretty quickly. I'm pretty sure they convinced themselves that they were going to have a substitute teacher for a bit, and I'd be back. It didn't matter how much I tried to convey the permanence of the situation. Their parents, who are also humans, understood that I am human as well. They all wished me the best and even gave me goodbye gifts! I keep in touch with some of them to this day.

My coworkers were no different. They had gotten to know me and my heart, and trusted that I was doing the right thing for myself. They even threw me the sweetest goodbye lunch party!

"I'm proud of you. You're taking life by the horns and doing what you need to do to be happy," I'll never forget a dear friend and teammate telling me. I learned so many valuable lessons in that situation.

Again, I learned that I can surprise myself and that nothing is impossible. I learned that I am in control of my own health and happiness. I can't, however, control how people react to my decisions. Therefore, I can't make decisions based solely on worrying about disappointing others. The funny thing is, I also learned that those times you worry that people will think you're crazy when you take a giant leap of faith, that worry usually doesn't pan out. The more common outcome is that they admire and respect you even more.

My last day was six weeks later, and it was the most bittersweet day. I remembered, six years earlier, that first day I'd walked into my very own classroom, right out of college and full of excitement. I had finally made it and achieved my longest-held life dream. I hadn't known what to expect, but I'd been so proud of myself.

But, there I was on my last day, packing up all my books and boxes full of little gifts my students had given me over the years. Picture frames with sayings like "World's Best Teacher" printed on them, a glass apple, and a folder full of every single picture or letter any student ever made for me.

My heart was full too. All two hundred fifty-nine students I had taught throughout my six years had a special spot in my heart forever, along with their families. My heart was full of so many sweet memories of those kiddos. Field trips and parties, lessons they loved, and even those they didn't, countless story times, the time one of them brought a real-life frog to school in their backpack.

## The Power of Quitting

It hit me that another one of my dreams died that day. Only this time, it was my choice. I reminded myself, though, that I could always go back to teaching. It would always be there for me. But, would this new dream wait for me? I wasn't sure, and I didn't want to risk it. So, while it was hard to close the door of my classroom, I knew it was going to allow me to open the door of a new, exciting dream.

Teaching was my dream job, and it served me well. But, I'd come to a point where it felt like it was holding me back from something bigger. I felt as though I were in a box, and when I quit, that box opened and I caught a glimpse of what else might be out there for me. I had no clue what it could be, how I'd get there, and no clue who I'd be if I wasn't a teacher. And I was going for it anyway.

Everyone back in Colorado was very surprised by the news that I quit. I was always told that I was the quintessential kindergarten teacher. But, I was so ready to show the world that there was much more to me than that. Even more so, I was ready to prove that to myself.

It's funny how sometimes we tell ourselves that we can only have one dream in life, which makes no sense. It's acceptable and actually encouraged for us to change and grow throughout life, so why wouldn't our dreams grow and change too?

A part of me felt like I was giving up, though. It was a similar emotion to how we'd felt about ending our time in Raleigh sooner than expected. For a minute, I went down that same path of feeling like a failure. But, as I reflected back on my six wonderful years of teaching, I remembered the impact I made. To this day I still hear from parents of students that I am their child's favorite teacher. They often tell me that their child still talks about me and remembers things I taught them.

How could I feel like a failure? I have full confidence that I didn't give up on my teaching dream. I gave it my all, and it will forever be a part of who I am. It helped shape me into who I am today. I hope I continue inspiring my former students to never stop chasing their dreams, even when those dreams change. I want to show them that changing dreams means that you're growing and improving.

Quitting teaching and leaving Raleigh taught me a lot about fear too. I had built up so much anxiety about quitting that I'd nearly made myself sick. All those scenarios I was playing out in my head? None came true!

It taught me that fear is nothing more than lies I tell myself because of my insecurities and uncertainties with the unknown. My fears are not a valid representation of what the future holds for me. I wasn't going to let fear steal every ounce of hope, confidence, and excitement I had for my new dream and future.

After moving to Raleigh, quitting my job, and making the decision to full-time RV, I felt like I had pushed fear to the backseat. "If I can do those things, I can do anything," I remember thinking. The more I pushed back on my fears, the more confident I felt to keep facing them. I had never felt so powerful in my entire life, and I couldn't wait to go out and see what the open road had for us. I felt like nothing could stop us!

### Item 2: Getting Out of the Lease

Well, we did have one little thing holding us back. It was time to move on to the second task on our to-do list . . . getting out of our apartment lease. So, we got permission to sublease our unit and find tenants to take over our rent payment! Perfect! We put out a bunch of ads and spread the word everywhere we could. But, we only got . . . crickets.

Meanwhile, we began selling as much of our belongings as possible, so we didn't have to haul as much back to Colorado. Most of it was going to sit in storage anyway.

However, downsizing turned out to be way harder than we'd thought it would be. I placed so much sentimental value in my teaching supplies and the furniture we'd purchased for our first house. We also wanted to hold on to so many things "just in case RVing didn't work out." But the more we sold, the more money we made, so we kept finding new things to sell. It became kind of addictive seeing all our clutter disappear.

We even got rid of both of our cars. We sold one and traded in the other for a truck. We decided when we got back to Colorado, we'd buy a fifth-wheel to be our rolling home and would need a truck to tow it.

We were slowly chipping away at that to-do list, one by one, but still we hadn't found tenants for our apartment. We decided we would be willing to lower the rent and pay the difference each month until the lease was up. This wasn't ideal—paying a couple hundred dollars to not live in an apartment—but we wanted this so badly that we were willing to do whatever it took, and it worked! Low and behold, right in the knick of time, we found the perfect renters.

We were officially free!

Days later we were driving a U-Haul truck across the country again, but this time with Raleigh in the rearview mirror. We had a thousand things running through our heads and what seemed like a million things left on our to-do list. But, I felt like a ton of weight had been lifted off of my shoulders. We had no idea what to expect and were a little scared that we were making the wrong decision. But, we knew we'd never regret giving this dream a chance, in the same way we didn't regret moving to Raleigh.

## Your Turn: From Dead End to Detour

I want this chapter to remind you or assure you that nothing is impossible. That anything is possible. When it comes to improving your situation, it's always worth whatever you have to go through to make it happen. You're not stuck. Is it time for you to close a door, so another can open?

Don't worry about the timeline you've set for your life. Don't worry about what others will think. Your situation doesn't define you; it's how you choose to react that does. It's your job, no one else's, to find your happiness and become who you're meant to be. Are you ready to quiet your fears and go for it?

When you start to dream of something new, you might get overwhelmed with fear. Try asking yourself, "What's the worst that could happen?" Will you die? Will the world end? Sure, there might be a few less-than-desirable outcomes. But, the worst-case scenario that you really need to ask yourself is "Will I regret not going for it?" Are you okay with playing it safe instead? It's up to you, but never believe that you don't deserve happiness. You are worth the risk.

The following chapter will inspire you to keep pursuing yourself, your detour, and your happiness. It will pay off, as you'll start to see it did for Dan and me. I was so proud and so glad that I found the courage to believe in myself and fight for myself, and I promise, you will be too! My detour finally led me to the beginning of a whole new journey.

Part Three

# The Journey

# 8

## The Open Road

*And He said, "My presence will go with you, and I will give you rest."*

—Exodus 33:14

Returning to Colorado, we couldn't help but feel like sad puppy dogs with our tails between our legs. We had full confidence in our hearts that we were doing the right thing. We knew Raleigh had been exactly what we needed to move ourselves forward. But, we'd get caught up worrying about what we must look like to others from the outside looking in.

Now, we're moving into an RV? Is that a step forward or backwards? We didn't quite know, and by the looks on the faces of the people we told, it was clear no one quite understood us either.

We were pretty certain people were thinking we were running from our problems. To be honest, in a way, we were. We figured, if we couldn't have kids, we'd do something we wouldn't be able to do if we did have kids. Besides, I did need a break. In my heart, I secretly did want to escape for a little.

I knew I couldn't run away from the facts of our situation or the pain I was still experiencing. I wanted to run towards what I knew would bring some joy back in our lives. I knew the undeniable feeling of happiness that traveling and exploring brought us. When it came to describing those feelings to others, though, we struggled.

"It's a new adventure!" was about all we could say whenever someone asked us why we decided to full-time RV. That question was too loaded, but at the same time, the simplest and best answer was "Why not?"

We had no clue where the road would lead us. We also didn't care, to be honest. The only thing we knew was that RVing would allow us the time to be together, just the two of us, to do what we love most. Nothing else mattered at that time.

We were open to whatever came our way but also didn't have a whole lot of expectations. Our only goals were to simplify, have fun, and be open to what God had for us. In a way, we had given up everything—most of our belongings, my job, the idea of stability, a house, our plans—to see what we could gain.

## Making It Official

Shortly after returning back to Colorado, we flew out to Austin, Texas, to attend an RV summit. The event was organized by the couple behind the podcast we'd been listening to. We felt a little nervous attending the event as "RVers" when we were really just "dreamers." But, we figured it could be a good way to learn about the lifestyle and meet some like-minded people.

The day before we flew out for the event, we purchased our first fifth-wheel for ten thousand dollars cash off Craigslist. Not even knowing what to check for, all we could do was pray that everything worked! We figured Dan would learn to tow it and operate it somehow, some way, when we returned from our trip. Because of the purchase, it meant that arriving at the summit, we could officially say we were "RVers" . . . right?

We pretended to know a lot of the RV terms that were being thrown around that weekend—rig, black tank, inverter, chassis, coach, boondocking. Turns out, it didn't even matter. It was the most welcoming group of people we had ever met. We instantly felt like we "belonged" and were surrounded by people who understood us, were just like us, and who "got it." For once, we didn't have to try and find the words to explain what we were feeling.

It couldn't have been better timing, and we left so encouraged and inspired. We didn't feel we were hitting the road alone any longer. We now had people all over the country, on wheels, that we could turn to for help, should we need it.

We came back from Texas with so much excitement and energy! When Dan and I set our minds on something, we go after it with full force and full speed. This was exactly what we needed to complete the rest of that to-do list and the challenges each task continued to bring us. Luckily, my uncle and Dad taught us everything—okay, almost everything—we needed to know about our new home. Our dads also helped us do some slight renovations to make the RV more livable, along with a few repairs too.

As silly as it seemed, we felt just as proud of that old RV as we did our first home in the suburbs. It was ours, and no matter where we took it, it was going to keep us safe, warm, and together. That was all we needed. Six weeks later, on April 8, 2017, we were officially on the open road as full-time RVers.

## Murphy's Law

That first day on the road was a doozy. Luckily, my dad came along with us for two weeks because we definitely needed supervision. The adventure began immediately. On our first stop to fill up gas, we accidentally left the tailgate of our truck down. This resulted in stuff flying out of the truck bed and onto the highway, nearly causing my dad to wreck his truck and trailer behind us. Hours later when we stopped for lunch, we discovered our refrigerator vent had flown off the roof. We realized that all along it had been duct taped on by the previous owner! Everything that could've gone wrong, went wrong. We were total newbies and, quite frankly, a hazard to others on the road.

My dad must've felt terrified to leave us as his two-week trip came to an end. The days following, we continued to have bad luck. Dan ran over his laptop with our truck, and I towed for the first time through California traffic with a broken trailer brake cord. Since it was my first time towing, I didn't realize that stopping shouldn't be *that* hard!

We also got stuck in a tight spot blocking traffic and needed a stranger to help us get out. Oh, and our spare tire on the back of the fifth-wheel fell off, luckily in a gas station parking lot and not on the highway. I should also clarify that all those things happened in one day! One horrible, terrible, no good, very bad day!

Something else happened that day. I sat on a curb and cried as I told Dan I didn't think we could do this. As I've made very clear so far in this book, I always look for "signs." Well, these signs were definitely telling me to give up.

"Remember, the shepherd boy in the book *The Alchemist*?" Dan asked as he attempted to cheer me up. "He got tested as he pursued his personal legend. This is the universe testing us, and we have to keep fighting." Dan spoke such powerful words there on that curb.

*The Alchemist* was a huge inspiration to us while making the decision to pursue RV life. It still is, to this day, our favorite book. So, just like the shepherd boy, we picked ourselves up and kept fighting through that day from hell. We somehow arrived safe and sound at our campground.

To our surprise, our site had no water or electricity. We'd missed this tiny detail when making the reservation. It was the cherry on the top of that day, but we were just happy to have arrived safely. It also didn't hurt that our site, despite its lack of hook-ups, was right on the beach. We could hear the ocean from our front door! So, we brushed it all off, grabbed some wine, and walked down to the water.

That night, we watched one of the most spectacular sunsets we'd ever seen.

"We're gonna be alright," we told each other under the fiery pink and orange sky. We had our feet in the sand, and our arms wrapped tight around each other.

The next day, we found out we were "coincidentally" parked next to a guy who was an electrician. He had worked on nuclear submarines in the Navy, back in the day. Needless to say, he graciously helped Dan fix the trailer's brake cord. He also loaned us his generator, so we could have power. He was, what I later discovered, our first of many "road angels."

We got much better at life on the road after that. We learned to slow down, for starters. On travel days, we'd go over our checklist three times and then say the same prayer together before we hit the road:

> Lord, we pray for calm bodies and clear minds, so we can stay alert and focused at all times, and make safe choices. We pray for ourselves on the road and others with us. We ask for safe weather and driving conditions, so we can arrive safely at our destination. Above all, we thank you for blessing us with this opportunity and for your love, guidance, and protection.

It became almost robotic we said it so often, but we knew we needed Jesus to take the wheel!

## Reality

After about a month, reality sunk in that this was our life and not a road trip. That realization was equal parts exciting and terrifying. We had already traveled about two thousand miles and through four states. We couldn't believe all the fun we'd had in one short month.

While the lifestyle wasn't perfect, it was perfect for us and we loved it! There was so much to love ... and so much to learn to love. Like the fact that full-time RVing is really just a fancy term for full-time camping. The bugs, the outdoors, the lack of showers, the bathroom situation ... it's not all that glamorous.

The lifestyle required lots of adjustment too. That freedom we were seeking was a blessing and a curse. We had to learn how to balance being on vacation with real life when it came to work and play. Living like you're on vacation full-time, we learned, isn't great on your budget, waistline, or productivity. It's a heck of a lot of fun, but not sustainable. Therefore, we had to find somewhat of a routine in a life where we wanted to get away from routine.

Learning new roles within our relationship was another challenge we faced in this new life. We each had our own specific tasks around the RV. I'll just say, I was happy to do pretty much everything except empty the tanks. We also had to get into a few arguments in order to establish these new roles, which was unusual for Dan and me.

Communication became more important than ever before. We talked about everything, and we talked a lot. We'd have long travel days and talk the entire drive. Sharing our struggles, dreaming up new ideas . . . we'd talk until there was nothing left to say. It reminded me of those days we'd sit and talk on the couch in our coffee room. It felt good to have those conversations again.

## Togetherness

RVing, even after only a few weeks, brought us so much closer together. Not just physically, being together in under two hundred square feet for twenty-four hours a day, but also emotionally. We were working towards a similar goal with this lifestyle. For so long we had been doing very separate things with our jobs, hobbies, and goals. It was nice to be on the same page.

Fortunately, we've always loved being around each other as much as possible. The more time we spent together, the better we were. RVing, like Costa Rica, was proving to be a wonderful decision for our marriage.

We were spending so much quality time together. After wrapping up work for the day, we could leave the RV and within minutes, be doing our favorite activities—fishing, hiking, biking, brewery hopping. We used to have to wait for the weekends to have fun. Even worse, we used to have to drive an hour or more to get to where we could enjoy some of these activities.

There was honestly never a bad day in the RV despite the not-so-glamorous parts. Sure, we had struggles. It was still real life. But no matter what was going on around us, we could step outside our front door and be right in nature.

The best part was that the landscape outside our front door changed every week. We went from the middle of the desert in Arizona, to the sandy beaches of California, to the mountains of Montana, and everything between. While in Malibu, we even watched whales and dolphins from our back window!

We loved the simplicity that life in the RV offered too. It only took fifteen minutes to clean our entire home. We had the best backyard, but zero yardwork. Our biggest stressors were deciding our route and finding a spot to park. Or going to the laundromat and dumping and refilling our tanks. We spent our free time however we wanted, minus one simple rule . . . we'd try to never miss a sunset! We would enjoy seeing and exploring as much as we could, and when we got tired of one spot, we could move on to the next.

"Why doesn't everyone live in an RV?" we'd always say. We felt like we had found the secret to life. We weren't sure we would ever be able to go back to living in a house, after experiencing this kind of freedom. Our dogs even loved RVing. Wide open spaces to explore, more exercise, new smells . . . we were all happy campers!

I felt things I hadn't felt in a while, if ever. I was happy, at peace, and for once not worried about the future. I woke up every day feeling content right where we were. The only thing I had to "worry" about was which destination we'd go to the following week. The only thing missing was my family. I, of course, missed them daily, but I never once felt homesick.

It was everything I needed—a mental and emotional break! RVing seemed to be the perfect antidote for my broken spirit. My health was better than ever too. I was feeling more and more like myself again every day. I loved being in control of my time, rather than a slave to my job. I got to do normal things again, like cook meals and walk the dogs with Dan. The days of coming home after dark and being too exhausted to do much of anything were long gone. I was enjoying even the simplest of things!

It was almost overwhelming how much I was enjoying RVing. I felt like my heart was going to explode with all the places we were getting to see and things we were getting to do. Everywhere we'd go would become my new favorite place. I'd stick my head out the window right along with the dogs and look out in wonder every time we arrived somewhere new.

We'd pull up, park, jump out of the truck, and say to ourselves, "We're home!" I'll never forget the day I watched the sun rise over the Grand Canyon and then set over Lake Havasu. Or the day we decided to take a day trip to San Francisco. Or the night we lay on the roof for hours drinking wine and looking up at the stars.

We spent my birthday month (yes, I celebrate for a month, not just one day) all over California. We biked through wine country, hiked through towering redwoods, and strolled barefoot on every beach along the beautiful Pacific Coast Highway. For our anniversary, the following month, we were in our favorite city, Hood River, Oregon. We had a night we'll never forget with a moonlit dinner by the Columbia River. We spent Fourth of July watching fireworks from an inflatable boat in the middle of a lake after a full day of exploring Glacier National Park.

## Transformation

Our first three months of RV life completely blew us away. We returned to Colorado for a visit and loved that anytime we needed a break from the travel or missed our family, we could drive back there. Returning "home," though, we felt like completely different people.

In those three months, we had grown so much, and the road had taught us many valuable lessons. We weren't expecting there to be so many more benefits, other than the travel!

"How's your trip going?" our friends and family would ask. But, this wasn't a "trip" to us. In our minds and hearts, we were finally living! A trip would indicate that there was an end, but there was no way we could fathom stopping everything we were doing anytime soon. Once again, we were at a loss for words when sharing these emotions with others. It was hard enough for us to even understand what was happening inside ourselves!

For starters, we were learning how to be more present. Not a day would go by without me thinking about what I would've been doing if we were still in Raleigh. I'd instantly feel so much gratitude. I was so thankful that I got myself out of that difficult time and did what it took to get to this new incredible journey.

It helped me have hope that my future was only going to continue to get better. No longer worrying about every detail of our future allowed me to live more in the moment. I didn't want these memories in the RV and on the road to pass us by. I was soaking it all in, and every little thing about this new lifestyle was something to celebrate. "I'm so lucky," I'd tell myself several times a day.

Being on the open road also expanded our horizons. It made our world so much bigger, and when your world gets bigger, your problems seem to get smaller. When you take the time to get out of your "bubble," you look at yourself and your life with a whole new lens.

We remember feeling this way during our time in Costa Rica and throughout other international traveling we'd done. But, we didn't expect to have a similar experience traveling in our own homeland. It surprised us that traveling through America felt a little like traveling through Europe. Every state and region has a different way of life with different environments and attitudes.

In addition, we were meeting so many interesting and inspiring people. Everywhere we'd go, there'd be someone new who had their own unique story. We'd spend time chatting, and they'd each have a special way of making an impact on us.

Not everyone at the RV parks and campgrounds was living in a camper for "fun" or adventure, like us. We drove through areas with extreme poverty. There was something incredibly powerful about seeing Americans, "our people," have such disadvantages. We've always known how privileged we are. Especially in comparison to other parts of the world. But, this opened our eyes even more. It inspired us to volunteer where we could and try to give back to the cities and areas we visited. It also reminded us how small our struggles are.

In fact, those three months, we hardly even talked about our infertility situation. We'd bring it up because it was what we had become accustomed to talking about for months prior to RV life. But, neither one of us would carry on the conversation. We both would agree that we were doing okay, and there was no more discussion to be had beyond that. We were still fine with doing "nothing" about it quite yet.

RVing had become the greatest blessing and was bringing us so much joy and excitement. Some days it was actually hard to feel sad about the fact that we couldn't have kids. If we had gotten pregnant, we most likely would've never hit the road full-time in the RV.

The thought of missing out on this adventure of a lifetime was hard to imagine. For that reason, I became genuinely glad that the timing hadn't worked out the way we had wanted it to. I have the rest of my life to be a mom, but this—this was once in a lifetime!

We sort of thought, and assumed others did as well, that we'd do the RV thing for only a little while. We'd have a lot of fun, and then sooner rather than later, we'd decide to "settle back down" and go back to trying to start a family again. But, that was proving not to be the case. RVing had become the vehicle, figuratively speaking, for bringing us to an entirely new outlook on life and our future. There was no end in sight to this detour!

So, after a short visit home, we continued on our journey and headed the opposite direction this time. We drove almost as far east as you can and landed in Bar Harbor, Maine. We enjoyed several stops along the way, including two major bucket list destinations, Chicago and Niagara Falls!

## The Call

We were back to taking full advantage of our freedom. We were traveling to see as many states, sites, and parks as we could. But the day we arrived in Maine, after feeling like we'd never make it that far, we received a call from home: Dan's mom was having health issues. We knew we wanted and needed to go home to be with her.

A few days later, we turned around and headed home as quickly as we could. Up until that point, we hadn't thought about what we'd do if a family emergency came up while we were on the road.

Technically, there wasn't a need for a "family emergency plan." There wasn't even a decision to make. Nothing comes before family for us, and we both knew that if at any point we needed to return home, we would do so. In fact, it made us fall even deeper in love with the RV lifestyle we had built. Not only could we fulfill our travel dreams, but we could also go home at any time for however long we wanted or needed. If we were still living in Raleigh, we wouldn't have had that luxury.

Selfishly, though, we were a little scared at what this meant for us. We weren't sure how long we'd be off the road, and this news meant we were moving back to Colorado for an unknown amount of time. During the long drive back, this all began to sink in, and while nothing was more important than being with Dan's mom, it still worried us. The more we thought about it, the more it started to feel weird to say we were "going home."

Our meaning of home had drastically changed. We felt home everywhere, yet nowhere, all at once. Home wasn't necessarily a physical location anymore. Home was now wherever we parked, wherever we were together. The thought of being away from that feeling of home, to be home in Colorado, was hard to wrap our minds around. As you can imagine, it was hard for our families to understand as well. From their viewpoint, we were putting a pause on our "trip" or adventure. To us, it felt like much more than that.

Regardless, we had become more firm than ever in our belief that there's a reason for everything. This was just another detour, and we knew we were right where we were supposed to be, no matter how hard it was for us to stop traveling. I'll say it again, nothing was more important than being with Dan's mom . . . nothing!

When we finally made it back to Colorado a week later, our RV was completely falling apart. The backend was starting to separate from the frame, the awning had flown off somewhere in the middle of windy Kansas, and our bedroom window had shattered. Turns out, we had dragged that ole thing a few too many miles! But, we were back, safe, and with Dan's mom. We parked the RV in storage, grabbed our belongings, and knew we'd deal with it later.

Our time back in Colorado had its ups and downs. We wanted to be present with our family, but the longer we were off the road, the more we began to feel lost. We weren't even sure who we were anymore if we weren't traveling. Our days had gone back to feeling mundane. We were going back and forth between our parents' houses and struggling to find our own routine and space.

It sounds so silly now, as I write this, but we honestly felt as though we had hit the "pause button" on our life. We were happy to be home and wouldn't have had it any other way, but couldn't deny that deep down we were struggling.

We stayed positive, as best as we could, and knew that the road would still be there when we were ready again. The priority was Dan's mom's health, and we knew we'd never regret the time we got to spend with her. It was an honor to be supporting her through one of the most challenging seasons of her life as she had supported us through ours. It was also the holidays and a wonderful time to be home with family.

Meanwhile, we had to face the fact that our home on wheels wasn't going to make it much farther. We hadn't wanted to invest too much money up front into our first RV, not knowing whether we'd even like RVing or not. But by this time, we were ready to upgrade and make a bigger investment into this lifestyle we had fallen so much in love with.

## Meet Wanda

"How long do you really think you'll continue RVing?" our friends and family would ask as we were shopping for a brand-new motorhome, way out of our price range. Our answer was always "As long as it makes us this happy." And we pulled the trigger on a shiny new Winnebago that we named "Wanda." She had everything we needed to "wanda" around the country and fuel our "wanda-lust."

Wanda was a complete changeup! No more towing and a lot less space (five feet less, to be exact). But, much more peace of mind knowing that it was new and under warranty. We couldn't wait to launch the second year of our travels and took her out for a few weekend trips to break her in.

Dan's mom, being the strong woman she is, was back to good health in time for Christmas. We started off a new year with so much to be thankful for and look forward to. Before long, we were back on the open road with so much eagerness to see what was ahead of us. We didn't know it at the time, but our second year on the road was going to be twice as good.

It's hard to imagine experiencing so much joy after one of the hardest seasons of your life. It's crazy exciting to think about how much can happen in a year, or even less.

## Your Turn: From Dead End to Detour

Before I go further into my personal journey, I hope you've seen the value in choosing yourself and choosing to pursue things that make you feel alive. For you, it may not be travel. Maybe it's a certain kind of work or a hobby. Investing in a skill, taking it to a higher level, or learning a brand new one to challenge your comfort zone. Whatever it is, choose yourself by determining to go after it and fill your life with it. Take an inventory of the things that are bringing you down and impacting your quality of life. Eliminate those things to free up space for the good things.

Even if it feels or looks like you're trying to escape from your problems, that's okay too. In fact, why wouldn't you try to escape them? Would you rather continue to sulk in them and surround yourself with constant reminders of the pain they bring you? A break from it all might be exactly what the doctor ordered!

In fact, I believe God sometimes encourages us to take a break. If you're feeling tested as you anticipate what will come as you follow your detour, I encourage you to take the time to rest with God. Let Him do the hard work in your life and for your future. Then, in the meantime, find ways of enjoying the present and the beauty that will soon unfold right in front of you.

People likely won't understand you and your decision. Yes, your family included. You might even run the risk of feeling selfish. That's why, from my experience, finding community—meaning people that support you, people that "get it" and get you—that's everything.

No matter what you're facing right now or whether you think you'll "fit in," get out there and meet people. There's so much value in connecting with others. Especially those who are either living the way you want to be living or share a similar passion as you. You need people who understand you.

Family and friends, as much as they love you, don't always know how to support you. Sometimes it makes them feel safer if you stay the same, keep things the same, safer because then they don't have to worry about you. Something to keep in mind is that you need different people during different stages of your life.

The more you fill your life with what you enjoy, the more community you'll organically find. Then, before you know it, you'll feel energized and excited about where your journey is leading you. When you start stripping away the fears, the anxiety, and the negativity in your life, you start to find your truest self.

It sure didn't take me long to start finding myself. As my journey continued, I began surprising myself with the challenges I was both overcoming and seeking out. This next chapter is my favorite, as it shares my story of conquering my greatest fear. The transformation I was experiencing during this phase of my journey came down to one life-changing experience.

# 9

## Learning to Fly

> *But those who wait on the Lord shall renew their strength; they shall mount up with wings like eagles; they shall run and not be weary; they shall walk and not faint.*
>
> —Isaiah 40:31

The travel continued to be exhilarating as we set out for our second year on the road. We were having just as much fun, especially in Wanda, our new RV. Only something inside me was different this time.

Despite all the happiness around me, I hadn't realized something I'd been struggling with internally. I hadn't fully recognized the identity crisis I'd been battling since leaving Raleigh. Whenever we'd meet someone new, which was often, they'd always ask the same two questions: "Do you have any kids?" and "What do you do for work?" I never knew how to answer those questions. I felt like I hardly knew who I was. Better yet, I hardly knew who I wanted to be.

For so long, my identity was wrapped up in being a teacher. But now, I was no longer a teacher, nor was I the mom I thought I would be at this point in my life. When we first hit the road, I didn't even have a job or responsibilities. I had lost so much of my purpose. I had started to put pressure on myself, which led to a lot of anxiety about my future—not just our future, not just our detour and whether or not we'd someday have children—but me. Who was I?

Dan kept telling me to give myself a break. By moving into the RV, we had lowered our cost of living by a considerable amount, and his salary was enough. He didn't want me to feel any pressure and rush into a commitment with a job that I was unhappy with again. Yet, I couldn't help but feel restless and antsy to do something. I wanted to feel valued again. I wanted to contribute to our life and living out our dreams.

The issue—I didn't know where to begin. I hardly even knew what skills I had. Of course, excluding tying shoes and teaching spelling words by singing songs. Or breaking up five-year olds fighting by reminding them that "Sharing is caring." Okay, it wasn't quite that bad. The real problem was that I didn't know how my skills would translate. I didn't know what interests I had outside of teaching, and I didn't know where to begin to explore those things.

So I did what every millennial would do ... I started blogging! Because who *doesn't* have a blog these days? We started the blog a few months before hitting the road. Okay, *Dan* started the blog, I can't take credit for its early stages. After naming our situation a "detour," there on the couch that day, he purchased the domain FollowYourDetour.com. At the time, we had no idea what we'd do with it. We always thought it would be cool to have a travel blog since we were often asked for travel advice and recommendations.

The problem was, we had tried the blogging thing back in Costa Rica (before blogging was even cool, mind you) and we were terrible at it. Our website was, https://sites.google.com/site/mckenziesgreatadventures. Yes, it's still up and quite embarrassing. It was basically a collection of letters home about how many monkeys we'd seen that day. That blog lasted a few short months, so, in my mind, I had completely written off blogging (see what I did there!). But Dan built the site anyway and did all the work to get it up and running and full of pages of our travels.

Since I had nothing better to do that first year on the road, I wrote. I kind of started to like it too. I started sharing our journey in as many ways as I could to who I thought was only our family reading it. My first post was about how quitting my dream job was a part of following my detour. It was uncomfortable at first. Putting all my business out there for anyone to see. I wasn't even sure I had anything valuable to share. I'd never considered myself a writer, and to be honest, I felt a bit like a phony. To my surprise, people other than just our parents began reading and subscribing to our blog. People I barely knew or didn't know at all came across it. I was getting comments and messages from friends and strangers alike saying they felt inspired by me. It was an amazing feeling.

So, I continued. I started writing about anything and everything. The "how-tos" of RV life, tips on the destinations we visited, and every so often I'd sprinkle in more personal stories about our detour. After regularly receiving great feedback on the site, by year two on the road, I decided I'd go all in and see how far I could take this little blog of ours. I went from "Lindsay the teacher" to "Lindsay the I-don't-know-what" and then claimed my newest title as "Lindsay the blogger." This was only the start of me discovering how multifaceted I am. I've since moved beyond that identity too. By the way, if you want to read our blog and see photos of our adventures, it's still up and running: www.followyourdetour.com.

When I started putting more of myself into our blog, I had no clue the greater impact it would have on me. It never crossed my mind that all the writing I'd been doing to more or less pass the time would actually be a pivotal part of the latest detour on the journey that I was about to embark on. A transformational detour filled with self-discovery that taught me exactly who I *really* am.

## "Lindsay the Entrepreneur"?

I started getting a variety of opportunities as a result of our blog. I landed freelance writing gigs for three major companies in the RV industry. I began working as a virtual assistant for several successful bloggers. And before long, I was collaborating with and even coaching other bloggers as well. I was hosting workshops, online webinars, and other virtual events. I was also being interviewed on other blogs and podcasts, and partnering with major brands.

I was "doing it," whatever that meant. Most of the time, I had no idea what I was doing at all, but I was willing to spend hours researching and learning anything I didn't know. I learned everything from web design, social media management, online marketing, email list management, and all the other million things that you're required to know as a blogger. Little by little, we turned our little blog into an actual business!

The day someone called me an "entrepreneur," I laughed and thought, "Not me!" I shrugged off the fact that within about a year of quitting my teaching job, I had replaced my income. I had done it by finding or creating my own work too. For whatever reason, there were still so many doubts in my mind that I could actually be successful.

Entrepreneur or not, I was so glad I put myself out there like I did through blogging, as uncomfortable as it was. I opened up about our story and our journey, the good and the bad. While it was hard at first, it connected me to a world of opportunities. Even better, it surrounded me with supportive, inspiring people.

It also became cathartic for me to write. It gave me purpose again, and in some small way, my writing was helping others. I had never realized how powerful it was to put my thoughts on "paper" (and now, here I am writing an actual book).

Blogging also helped me to start deeply believing in myself. Not just thinking that I could achieve things, but actually believing it and acting on it. I was slowly starting to build up my confidence and learn that with hard work and dedication, I could actually do whatever I wanted and be whoever I wanted.

## No Limit

I continued to push myself towards discomfort, knowing that it would help me learn and grow even more. I was challenging myself in a variety of ways, starting with running a half-marathon. Running was never my thing. In other words, I despised it . . . sort of like writing. I never would have imagined it would be physically or mentally possible for me to run 13.1 miles, but I did it. We did it! Dan and I ran the whole way, and when we crossed that finish line holding hands, I felt so accomplished and proud of myself.

Shortly after the race, we started getting filming opportunities. We got to be a part of a documentary by Vice Media. (It's called *American Dreaming*, if you're interested.) We were on the TV show *Going RV!* (Season 7, Episode 9, again if you're interested.) Our favorite, though, was getting to be the hosts of a web-based travel show called *The Happy Camper Bucket List* by Camping World!

I'm sure you guessed it, but being on camera—also, wasn't my thing. I've always been the reserved type and one to hide in the shadows. I'm sure you can also guess that I wound up loving it! Maybe it was this new confidence that I was gaining, but I found myself loving the energy I'd get from being in front of the camera. It was like I'd ignited a new spark inside me.

"Who am I?" I would catch myself thinking—but this time in the best way possible because I wasn't lost anymore. I was surprising the heck out of myself. I was seeking out anything that challenged me or made me question whether I was capable or not. I was completely rediscovering myself and loving who I was finding that had been hiding behind the walls I had built throughout my life.

## The Final Push

There was one final thing I needed to overcome. The day came that required me to really dig deep and let go of fear. The day I learned to move from simply spreading my wings, to actually flying . . .

Okay, so I didn't technically fly. But I conquered one of my all-time greatest fears . . . skydiving! I know that skydiving isn't a huge fear that interferes with your ability to chase your dreams. Yet, unless you've done it, you may not understand the metaphorical impact it had on me.

You see, I am terrified of heights. Actually, not only heights, but ledges and, specifically, falling from heights. I have those dreams where you slip off edges and wake yourself up from flailing your arms, almost nightly. I can't even walk near the railings at malls or go over bridges—in a vehicle— without getting a falling feeling in my stomach. I've grabbed strangers by the arm before because I've been too close to an edge. I'd get that falling feeling in my stomach and could've sworn I was going over . . . and no way was I going alone.

I can't emphasize my fear enough. And don't let our travel photos showing me standing on overlooks with my arms stretched out fool you. You wouldn't believe all that I went through—and Dan too!—to get those shots. So, when I got word that we were going skydiving in Key West, Florida, for the travel show we were hosting, I started preparing for my death.

I was certain I was going to have a heart attack the moment the door on the plane opened. I cried off and on the whole night before and the morning of. I wrote Exodus 33:14 on my palm because I needed God to "go with me" quite literally—I needed Him to jump out of that plane with me.

My mom told me, "You're braver than you think you are," which I repeated to myself over and over again.

My best friend chimed in to offer encouragement. "Just spread your wings and fly!" she told me. She has no idea what those words meant to me in that moment and the greater impact they would have as well.

When we moved to Raleigh, Dan's aunt gifted us a small wooden sign. It has a bird painted on it and reads, "Until you spread your wings, you'll never know how far you can fly." I remember looking at that sign as I pulled it out of a box after moving back from Raleigh. I hung it in our RV and remember thinking, "I'm so ready to spread my wings!"

During our detour, I had a strong connection to wings. I loved that they symbolized freedom and rising to new heights, both of which I was seeking.

Dan and I even incorporated a feather into our Follow Your Detour logo. This was partly because of our "You can't clip our wings" saying. Everywhere I'd look, it seemed there were wings reminding me to spread mine.

So, I'll never forget being pushed out of that airplane (yes, pushed!). I screamed, closed my eyes, and then felt my arms getting pulled apart. When I finally found the courage to open my eyes, the first thing I thought was: "I'm flying!!" My arms couldn't have stretched out any wider.

I've never before felt such exhilaration and joy in my life. I was soaring ten thousand miles above the ocean. Below me, the Florida Keys appeared like a painting of blues and greens, and I got lost in God's beautiful masterpiece. I screamed, "I love this!!" over and over again, and shockingly, I didn't want the parachute to open! When we made it to the ground, I never felt so alive! Once again, I did it! Now that I had proven to myself that I could fly, I realized there was nowhere I couldn't go

Skydiving was that final push for me. It taught me that I really am braver and stronger and more courageous than I think I am. Growing up, I was quiet, shy, and careful. I was fearful too, and I hated being out of my comfort zone. Everything I'd once believed about myself was proving to be untrue. Conquering my fears was helping me find the real me.

As I write this book, Dan and I are coming up on the end of our second year of RV travels, and I hardly recognize who I have become. I've accomplished things that I never would've imagined for myself. I've gained so many new skills and interests, and it couldn't be more exciting! I find myself not only willing to step out of my comfort zone and go after new ventures, but I'm approaching them with a confidence I've never known before.

I finally believe that I really, truly, seriously can be anything I want to be and do anything I want to do. I think back to who I was when I came to that dead end with our infertility—and I smile. I've come so far!

I've finally learned where my true identity lies. My identity has nothing to do with being a teacher or whether I'll be a mom or not. It's not about being a blogger or a traveler either. My identity is about believing in myself. It's about fighting for myself and knowing that I deserve and will achieve greatness. I've learned that my work or job or title (or lack thereof) doesn't define me. It's up to me to be the person I want to be in this world. I will make an impact in this world, just being me.

People often ask me if I miss teaching, and my answer is always yes. Yes, I miss that every morning I'd get greeted with a hug and hear a sweet little voice say, "Good morning, Mrs. McKenzie!" I miss seeing children's faces light up when they'd learn something new and knowing that it was because of me. I miss reading them stories and teaching them both to read and fall in love with books and the knowledge they hold. I could go on and on. Most of all, I miss being around the beautiful energy and innocence that children have. I've always said that those five-year-olds taught me more about life than I ever taught them.

But, then, I follow up with a no, I don't miss teaching. It turns out, I never quit teaching. I don't need to be in the confines of a classroom or sacrificing my own happiness and health to be a teacher. Teaching is my God-given talent, and I will always carry it with me, no matter where I go. I can teach anywhere or anyone. I can teach through my writing, I can teach my nieces and nephews, and every day I even teach myself new things! I'll always seek out ways to teach and, more importantly, ways of making an impact in others' lives.

I've experienced more growth in our second year of RVing than I ever have in my life.

It was this phase of our journey that I experienced the power of a detour. I turned some of the most painful news into the most beautiful season of transformation. I could've very well let that devastating dead end tear me down. I could've grown bitter and closed myself off to anything else life had to offer. But, instead, I viewed it as an opportunity. I embraced the possibility of something greater . . . and I'm sure glad I did.

I've achieved so much, but following my detour still makes me the most proud. Choosing to accept that my perfect plans weren't working and being willing to do whatever it took to find joy again entailed more courage than skydiving or anything else I've overcome. Without this detour, and especially without that dead end, I wouldn't be who I am today—the real me.

I wouldn't be the strong, brave, and fearless woman I am continuing to become. I wouldn't be writing this book, and I wouldn't be sharing this message with you. This detour of mine has been one of the greatest blessings. As we wrap up another year of traveling in the RV, we continue to feel amazed by where it's led us. As I share in the next chapter, you'll see how far the journey continues to take us.

## Your Turn: From Dead End to Detour

We tend to put labels on ourselves because of our past, our upbringing, or certain experiences. We believe things about ourselves that aren't true. These voices in our heads tell us who we are, what we deserve, what we're capable of, and where we're going. Actually, most of the time, these voices tell us who we aren't, what we don't deserve, what we can't do, and where we're not going. But, when you challenge yourself, face your fears, and step out of your comfort zone, you learn to stop believing those negative voices. They lose all their power over you. With those voices silent, you make room for the real you.

I encourage you, today, to first start opening up about what you're going through. Whether it's through writing, music, art, or something completely different—share your pain, your fears, your desires, your story. You never know where it will lead you. You also never know who needs to hear it and who you might help. It can be your first step towards discomfort as well as your start to gaining serious confidence in yourself.

After you make the decision to choose yourself and begin to follow your detour, it becomes more about the journey. This journey is where you learn to find your real self. Think about where your identity lies. Is it inside you or are you letting something define you that shouldn't? Or are you lost and not sure of who you are at all, like I was?

Either way, take action towards your own self-discovery even if you aren't sure which direction to go quite yet. Action will bring clarity. It's up to you to do what it takes to grow. It's time for you to spread your wings. Go after the impossible and prove yourself wrong. You are stronger and braver than you think you are. Believe that anything is possible for yourself, and eventually you'll learn to fly too . . . even if you have to be pushed.

# 10

## The Destination

*Commit to the LORD whatever you do, and He will establish your plans.*

—Proverbs 16:3

In wrapping up our second year on the road, it's taken a while to catch our breath. We can hardly keep up with all the traveling we've done. We drove twenty thousand miles through sixteen states this past year! We caravanned with RV friends to Canada and even crossed into Mexico. There were no boundaries with where we wanted to go! We even got to spend a little time in Europe.

Dan and I have been living the dream. I could go on and on about the beautiful sights we've seen or the moments we'll cherish forever. I could list off our favorite destinations and talk for hours about them. But again, year two of full-time traveling affected us in a completely different way.

It became less about how far and wide we traveled, and more about the deep journey of personal growth inside ourselves. On the road, we'd find ourselves feeling more inspired. We've become better versions of ourselves—more focused, intentional, and positive. Our goals shifted from exploring the country, to exploring bigger dreams for ourselves.

## Pedal to the Metal

Today, four years into the detour and two years into full-time RVing, for the first time ever, the two of us feel confident that we can go after anything. Not only for ourselves, but for our life together as well. Our time on the road has shown us exactly what we want in life. We want freedom and flexibility with where we are, how we spend our time, and the work we choose to do. The taste of freedom we've experienced during our time on the road has made us thirst for even more. Pursuing the RV dream has shown us the power of following our detour. The journey of our detour has allowed us to locate within ourselves the courage and confidence we need to keep going after more.

We've been through a lot. From the collapse of our original dream and plan, to leaving Colorado, then Raleigh, to hitting the road, and everything in between. Through it all, Dan and I have determined that fear could no longer hold us back. We've conquered it several times now. We aren't going to let it stop us from continuing to move forward in the direction of our growing dreams. We are now

## THE DESTINATION

feeling empowered to take bigger risks to achieve these dreams.

So, here I am again, with new, changing dreams. Now that I know that I can fly, the sky's the limit! Both Dan and I have always thought we were created for big things, but we believe that now, more than ever. We are so eager to continue on our journey to discover what else God has planned for us.

While we love RVing and plan to continue traveling as much as we can, we have an even greater vision now. We have a vision of a life that we used to be convinced wasn't achievable for "average people like us." A life where there are no limits and no pressure to live a certain way. A life filled with the time and resources to do even more of what makes us happy. But also the ability to bring happiness to others too.

We've been brainstorming and envisioning everything that could be possible for us. One of our greatest dreams is to have online businesses. Businesses we can operate from anywhere, whether we are "home" in Colorado or across the world, in say, New Zealand, Bali, or South Africa. We also seek more than simply jobs or work. We aim for projects we're passionate about. Projects that could bless other people's lives.

## Dream Pursuit

We're already taking steps towards that dream. In fact, Dan recently quit his full-time corporate job! We never imagined we'd have had the "cojones" to give up the security and salary Dan's job offered us.

But, we're willing to sacrifice anything to go after this dream of ours.

We launched an exciting new business that we're thrilled about. It's called Nomad Collab, and I'll explain it in the coming paragraphs. During our time on the road, we've come across many other couples living a similar lifestyle as us. Many also shared the same goals and values as us and it was as if we had an instant connection to one another. A deeper connection and bond than we'd experienced with other couple friends.

There were two couples in particular that we formed a "mastermind" with. We began having bi-weekly video calls where we'd share our successes and struggles, set business and personal goals together, and hold each other accountable. Since the road can often get lonely and navigating the challenges of this lifestyle can be tricky, this little community we built became critical to pursuing these new dreams of ours.

Knowing that there were so many other couples out there that likely needed this same support network, we decided we'd expand! We wanted to offer the benefits we'd gotten from our group to other nomadic and driven couples just like us. Other than the popular social media channels, there was nowhere for such like-minded couples to connect. We had a vision for a place that could serve as a one stop shop for everything you need to know about building a nomadic lifestyle. A little space on the internet where us "crazies" could support and learn from one another, collaborate together, swap ideas, and most important, have digital and in-person meetups, no matter where we were on the map! Since it didn't exist, we built it, and Nomad Collab was born. If you want more information, head over to NomadCollab.com.

We work much harder these days to grow our businesses and ensure we have enough each month to survive, and we love it. We work longer hours than ever, many of which see very little "financial return," but we have full freedom now. We don't have to juggle our travel with paid time off. We don't have to be glued to our computers during normal business hours. If we want to live abroad for a few months, nothing's stopping us. Our work will go with us wherever we go. It will fit into our lives, rather than us trying to fit time for our life around our work, as we used to do.

We may or may not have success with our businesses, but we know for a fact, we won't fail if we give it a shot! Failing doesn't apply. It's about growing, transforming, and learning.

We've also started dreaming of owning a home base in Colorado. Yes, you read that correctly! We're dreaming of owning a house again where we could live when we aren't traveling and want to be near family, and that we could rent out when we're away. A home base would also allow us to explore the option of adopting a child. Apparently, a traveling RV isn't considered a home when it comes to doing a "home visit," who knew?

We never used to allow ourselves to dream quite so big. We felt guilty for wanting so much. We used to feel we needed to choose one or the other: stability or freedom, home or travel. But now we no longer look at these pursuits as contradictory. We feel bold enough to chase one dream *and* another simultaneously. We don't have to limit ourselves, and we believe we have what it takes to make anything our reality.

That guilt we felt for wanting "and" instead of "or"—we acknowledged that was simply fear and insecurity trying to creep back in. We've had to fight back against those voices of doubt. With a little courage, we've already come this far. Now, we know it's only a matter of getting out of our own way and reminding ourselves that "you can't clip our wings." So, we're going full speed towards these visions with sheer determination.

For so long we'd let our limiting beliefs stop us from going all in on life. We told ourselves we could never move to another city and be away from our family, but we did it. We told ourselves that full-time travel was only for the rich, famous, or retired. Yet, here we are. So, why stop now? Why not believe that we can grow successful businesses? Why couldn't we have a dream home and still travel whenever we want? Why not continue to pursue all this and believe that someday, we'll figure out how to grow our family too?

This shift in us and in our thinking has been tremendous. Following our detour has shown us that the possibilities are endless. We don't have to stick to one path, and we definitely don't need a map with directions. We can pave our own roads and choose any route we want. Dead ends won't stop us, they'll take us on more detours. Those detours will then guide us towards a more exciting part of our journey.

## There's No Going Back

As I write this book, it's been four years now since we followed our detour. I used to tell myself I would write a book after we got "through" the detour. We'd have a child, or two, and we'd be "back on track." My thought was that I could write a story about staying faithful and patient on your detour. I'd share tips for waiting until your detour leads you back to whatever outcome you had been seeking initially.

In other words, I wanted our detour to be a loop, which would lead us back to that original road we were on. Sort of like a long roundabout way of still getting to where I'd wanted to go. But, since we started following our detour, we've taken other detours along our journey. Now, we've come so far that there's no chance of going back to that original path.

Today, I'm nowhere near where I was before. I don't have children. We still don't even have the slightest clue if we'll ever have any. It still hurts at times too. I still ask God almost daily what the heck He's waiting for and what He has planned. But regardless, I love this path I'm on right now. I've loved every step along the way, even the painful parts.

With how much I've grown, I don't want to go back where we started. That would be like turning around and going backwards. I'm a new me with new dreams and desires. I have a whole new outlook and attitude. I'm eager to keep going forward and exploring the unknown. Dan and I now seek out new detours to take any chance we get along our journey. We embrace change and challenges in our lives, and know that endings bring about beautiful beginnings. From Dan quitting his job to me writing this book, our eyes are always open for new opportunities, and it seems there's new detours waiting around every corner for us.

In many ways, today is just the beginning of our journey. Which is crazy to say considering where we are now is a result of that initial heart-breaking dead end. But our journey, while painful and lonely at times, shaped (and continues to shape) us into who we are today.

## Breaking the Cycle

I am confident in my belief that I had to experience everything along the way. Every part, good and bad, helped me become who I am now and the person I am still growing into every day. Even though I'm still going through it, I'm so much more prepared and ready for whatever God has in store for me. I can feel Him shaping me and my heart.

I recently went back to that favorite Bible verse of mine, Psalm 37:4. "Delight yourself in the Lord and He will give you the desires of your heart." This time, I read it with a completely different lens. I found that I was no longer angry at God for not giving me the greatest desire of my heart, to be a mother.

This time I chose to read it as God will be the provider of those desires. If I find delight in Him and His plans, He will put the desires He has for me in my heart. Over the past four years, He has given me new desires that I never would've chosen for

## THE DESTINATION

myself. Wonderful desires that I used to think were too big for me, until I followed my detour.

While I still have the desire to be a mother, I sense more than ever that God will fulfill that in His way and His timing. My prayer is that He will change my heart and continue to help me desire the way He wants me to receive that child. I've given up secretly hoping the detour is a loop, and I fully embrace it as a journey in which the outcome is not in my control nor of my making. I've given up my perfect plans for my life to Him now.

I'll be the first to admit that this is much easier said than done. When we first found out we couldn't conceive, I absolutely didn't want to embrace an alternate path. I didn't think anything else could make me happy.

Instead, I resisted it and rushed towards plan B, the option that was the next best thing. Which I don't regret. In fact, it played a critical part in following our detour. But, I kept thinking, "Once we get a baby, it will all be okay." Except, if we had gotten a baby out of it, would I really be okay? Or would I be thinking about baby #2 or wishing for the next thing in life . . . a new house or job?

For a long time, Dan and I had been going along this journey basing our happiness on achieving our desires. We'd convinced ourselves that if we could have _____ [insert desire], then we'd be happy. But, it doesn't work that way. We get _____ [a desire] and then we want _____ [next desire in line]. Let me lay out all the "If we could have _____" situations we've put ourselves through:

- If we could have a *baby*, then we'd be happy.

- If we could have a *change of scenery*, then we'd be happy.
- If we could *live and travel in an RV*, then we'd be happy.
- If we could have a *home base and a thriving business*, then we'd be happy.

Shall I go on?

No, you get the point.

It's a never-ending cycle because the more we gain, the more we desire. I don't think there's anything wrong with that, though. We'll always be striving for more and for better. We're human! As I've said throughout the book, the more we change and grow, the more our dreams and desires change and grow with us. But, delaying our true happiness until we acquired those things was where we got it wrong.

This has been the greatest lesson for Dan and me along our journey. We've learned that contentment doesn't come from getting what you want out of life. All this time we've been chasing after our happiness and fulfillment. Thinking it would be at the next destination or at the end of our journey. We've finally realized that happiness and fulfillment aren't destinations. It's been inside us the whole time, and all we had to do was find it.

That's why today, Dan and I are *choosing* to be happy and feel fulfilled. We're finding happiness in every part along our journey, the good and the bad. We're no longer rushing to find it in a destination that doesn't necessarily exist. In fact, as I write this book, we aren't currently traveling in our RV. We also haven't fully achieved most of those dreams I mentioned above. Some might look at us and think there's no way we could be truly happy. But, actually, we have more happiness than we've ever had before.

The secret? Fulfillment comes not from gaining everything you desire. Sure, we found happiness as we traveled and explored new places. We found happiness in the experiences we gained and the memories we made. But our true happiness and fulfillment didn't come until we started experiencing the changing and moving happening inside of ourselves. Fulfillment comes from the personal growth you gain along the journey of your detour.

Following our detour has had little to do with the physical locations it's led us to. The power of a detour was and always will be in the transformation that happens when you push yourself out of your comfort zone and say yes to the unknown. So, for us, whether we're staying in our parents' basements, in an ocean-view rental somewhere in Tahiti, or in our RV in Yellowstone National Park, we're happy because of who we are today. We're fulfilled because our detour allowed us to find who we *really* are and discover that our desire to grow and improve ourselves outweighs our desires to travel, be successful, or even become parents.

We know we'll continue to have hard times. Our journey won't be perfect, and life will continue to bring seeming dead ends, little bumps, and even deep ruts and unforeseen potholes. We may or may not feel happy and fulfilled throughout every phase.

But, even in our struggles, we can look at each other and instantly know that everything's going to be okay. It's like we have our own little secret way of going back in our minds and reliving all the beautiful moments along our detours that wouldn't have been possible without our difficult nos, nones, and nothings. We know we'll always have that to fall back on, as a source of peace in any situation.

For that reason, we'll continue to seek out detours and do all we can to embrace them. We know that each one will allow us to grow and find our happiness. Not because of where it will take us, but because of how it will shape us. And I hope you already realize that everything I'm saying here about Dan and me applies to you too. It's for all of us. The detour mindset is available to anyone.

## Your Turn: From Dead End to Detour

Our desires guide our every move in life. When we laser-focus ourselves on the pursuit of a desire, we get tunnel vision, living each day and planning out our lives solely to achieve that desire. What we might miss out on, though, are the opportunities that God has for us along the way, opportunities that may be disguised as nos, nones, and nothings. God is a much greater author of our plans. While He will fulfill your desires at the most perfect time, He also has even greater desires and plans for you that reach so far beyond your limiting beliefs and fears, that you aren't aware they are possible for you—yet.

He created you. He knows you. He wants to give you everything and more! Don't miss out on those opportunities because of the pain or the dead end of your own plans, which often don't materialize.

Don't miss those detours either. They aren't on your tiny map; they are on God's master design and will lead you on the most incredible journey imaginable. He will align your desires with His and adjust your plans accordingly.

When we give up control, even when it's the hardest thing ever, we open ourselves up to receiving God's possibilities and widening the pathways to fulfilling our desires. And, as a result, eventually, our purpose becomes more clear. At the same time, through our personal growth, we're able to find happiness and fulfillment again. When we choose the detour mindset and truly open ourselves up to God's greatness, beautiful life experiences unfold for us.

Remember to choose happiness no matter where you are along your detour, whether summiting a mountain and taking in the sweeping views, or in the depths of a valley with no clear direction or way out. Your happiness is right where you are. Right inside you.

Find your happiness and fulfillment in every step of the journey. If you're rushing, looking for satisfaction in the things you might gain in the future, or waiting to reach the supposed destination, you'll never find it. Your journey never ends, and there's no real destination. You'll always be moving, always looking for more. If you seize the opportunities to challenge yourself and learn new things, you'll find your happiness in the growth you undergo with every risk you take, fear you overcome, and desire you achieve.

As you fulfill these desires, though, remember to appreciate the journey you took to get there.

Celebrate who you've become. Celebrate your new desires and dreams. Then, continue on your way with appreciation for your "dead end" and "failed plans." Without them, your detour couldn't have been possible.

The next and final chapter outlines the "detour mindset." It lays out the key beliefs that Dan and I have learned throughout our incredible journey, and the attitudes we've adopted, which have been critical in finding our happiness. My aim with the final chapter is to provide a go-to reference when you need a little guidance or inspiration to embrace your detour, whether the road is smooth or bumpy . . . well . . . *especially* when it's bumpy!

# 11

# The Detour Mindset

The detour mindset I'm sharing in this chapter has absolutely changed my life. We call it the "detour mindset" because these perspectives and beliefs will help you find the courage to follow your detour. In fact, this mindset will help you with every step along the way. It will help you turn that dead end into the greatest story and journey of your life.

This mindset, laid out in seven principles, will prepare you to find your true happiness, no matter where you're coming from, where you're at currently, or where you're headed. So, let's jump in!

## #1: It's all about your perspective.

When we come to the dead ends in life, or when we become desperate for a change, it's easy to feel sorry for ourselves. Sure, our pain and fears are heavy in those moments, but we were never promised that life was going to be easy. Time and time again, life proves to be unfair, and not everybody gets an equal share of hard times. The only guarantee in life is that you're given the choice in how you respond to these events.

So, will you choose to soak in your self-pity and anger, or rise above it and seek out the meaning behind it?

Is your life *really* falling apart, or is it the start of it falling into place?

Take a moment to consider the fact that God could be turning your mess into a masterpiece. This could be exactly what you needed to happen for you to realize the blessings that lie ahead.

Your perspective is everything when it comes to choosing your happiness. Shifting your perspective is also the most important step in adopting the detour mindset. Without changing the way you look at your situation, it's impossible to experience the power of a detour.

## #2: There's always something to be grateful for.

In my experience, the quickest way I found (and continue to find) peace in the depths of my pain, was by having an attitude of gratitude. As shared in chapter 4, I finally started looking beyond that one area in my life that wasn't going as planned: Dan's and my inability to have biological children together. As well as my brother's early death. In doing so, I was able to see all the great things that had happened and were happening.

I went almost thirty years of my life without any major pain or disruption in my plan. That's pretty incredible! I realized how sad it was that I was choosing to focus my energy on the things that hadn't worked out the way I wanted.

Are you choosing to focus on that one unhappy thing? That incredibly disappointing hurt? . . . Can you dig deep and look beyond? Even for a moment?

Having gratitude in the darkest moments in life isn't easy. However, it will come a bit more naturally with that shift in perspective (remember, principle #1).

For example, take my brother's early and unfortunate death. It was a dark, dark time for me. At first, I couldn't find any blessing in losing him at such a young age. But, as I opened up and found the courage to look beyond, I discovered that many people around me weren't close to their brothers because of their differences. I had a great relationship with my brother, he taught me so much about life in the twenty-eight years we had together, and he left me with many amazing memories, enough to last a lifetime. I've chosen to be grateful for those things rather than holding on to my anger of losing him.

Another thing that helps is reminding myself, "It could always be worse." When I focus on the ways my situation could be more painful, it helps me find the silver lining in anything. Take a moment to look around and chances are you'll see that some people actually do have it worse than you.

Every single day I practice pointing out what I'm grateful for. I find gratitude in things that happened that day or things that are an everyday part of life that I often overlook. The more you practice being grateful, the more natural it becomes. It shifts your focus to what you *do* have rather than what you *don't* have.

FOLLOW YOUR DETOUR

## #3: Live in the now, and don't worry about the how.

The hardest part of finding the courage to follow a detour is not having any idea of where it will lead you. Throughout the book, I described how lost Dan and I were. Not only in the beginning of our detour, but throughout it. I wanted a map or a compass so badly. I searched for "signs" or bread crumbs . . . something to help me understand how to get where God wanted us to go. I was so stuck living in the future that at times, I missed out on the beauty of the journey.

Even when you have faith that your future is bright, the unknown can still cause so much anxiety. This anxiety can turn into paralysis when it comes time to move forward after a devastating dead end. Moving forward often involves change, and change often requires a series of decisions. We approach decisions based on how they will impact our future. But, when our plans get shattered and we no longer have a clear vision of the future, it's even more tough to make decisions.

It's likely you'll create hypothetical situations or "what-ifs." Many times, these "what-ifs" create terror-inducing images in your mind. You imagine your decision leading to the worst possible outcome. But typically, those worst-case scenarios rarely come to fruition. I'll talk more about this in principle #5, "You are Bigger Than Your Fears," below.

Dan and I are known for being some of the most annoying decision-makers. We like to know every single option and weigh out every possible outcome before we make any decision, including a Taco Bell order. So, take my advice on decision-making with a grain of salt!

There's one thing I've learned, for sure (other than the best Taco Bell order is a cheesy gordita crunch and a steak quesadilla!). I've learned that God is greater than our decisions. He is also so loving that He gives us choices, despite knowing that we often screw up. That's why we have to make decisions the best we can with the information we do have in the moment. It helps to know that even if it's the wrong one, we won't screw up God's plans and we can course-correct with His guidance. He's accounted for our mistakes or wrong decisions in His sovereign plans for our lives. We can have peace knowing that He's got our backs!

For now, though, the only decision you need to make is to trust God. He will reveal the how. Then, take action in the direction of your dreams. You don't need to think about how you'll get there. You only need to focus on what you can do today that will get you one step closer.

It's also important to note that living in the *now* means you can't worry too much about the future, but you also can't be held back by your past. It's nearly impossible to embrace the growth and power of a detour if you're constantly looking back with regret. Wishing you would've done something differently and wondering where you could've been if you had will take you nowhere. In fact, it will make you feel stuck in those dead end moments. You'll be too fearful to follow your detour because you'll worry about making the same not-so-great decisions or mistakes. Remember, you can't screw up God's plans. In fact, there might have been a valuable lesson you needed to learn from your past regrets. He might even use those not-so-great decisions we sometimes make for His good, somehow, someway.

Regarding the paralysis that rehashing the past or worrying about the future can lead to—I still sometimes catch myself worrying that Dan and I "gave up" too soon with the IUI. Which then leads to me wonder if we'll ever know the right time to try again or adopt. I also am regularly tackling what-ifs in my new role as an entrepreneur. I worry about missing out on opportunities, or I question whether we're doing the right things at the right times. I'm sharing this, so you'll know that realistically worry and what-ifs don't one day magically disappear. They continue, and they change as you change, but that doesn't mean you allow them to paralyze you. You recognize them for a quick moment—and more importantly, you act anyway.

It takes a lot of courage and commitment to live in the present, and it's not always easy, but the next principle will help you find the confidence you need to know you're on the right track.

## #4: Everything has its time.

To keep myself from dwelling on the past or feeling anxious about my future, I have to continually remind myself that everything has its time. Especially when it comes to a human life, in my situation, which is the greatest example of God's perfect timing. Here's the proof . . .

*Ecclesiastes 3:1–2 reads: To everything there is a season, a time for every purpose under heaven: A time to be born, And a time to die; A time to plant, And a time to pluck what is planted.*

It's nonsense to think that because Dan and I stopped trying IUI with the donor sperm, a baby wasn't born when it should've been. Or, that an opportunity that God had for me went to someone else instead because I didn't go looking hard enough for it. That's giving *me* all the power and taking it from our mighty God. I can't say it enough—we won't miss out on a single thing God has for us, we just won't!

I encourage you to stop every now and then, look back, and reflect on every step of your journey. Chances are, you'll be amazed by how perfectly everything worked out, even if it felt like total chaos at the time. I've actually noticed that there's always been a reason for those times when I thought I had made the wrong decision. It's like connecting the dots of your life . . . Because you did ____, you were led to ____, which brought you to ____.

I know I said not to live in the past, so to clarify, the only time you should look back on the past is to enjoy the view from how far you've come. I'll show you what I mean by using myself as the example: looking back, without the news that Dan and I couldn't conceive, we may have never moved to Raleigh. Without moving to Raleigh, we may not have sold our house at that perfect time, which led us to pay off our debt. Without paying off our debt and being unhappy with teaching, I may have never had the courage to quit my job. I had to quit my job, though, to pursue our new dream to travel. Traveling helped me discover new things about myself. It taught me invaluable lessons I'm sharing in this book now.

Looking back makes you realize how important every single dot is. Even the ones that are painful. I can say with confidence that receiving the news after Dan's surgery was the best thing that's happened to us. As I've shared, Dan and I believe we may have never gotten where we are now without those struggles we faced. Without them, we wouldn't have experienced our detour. We had to go through those struggles to get here today. We have more hope and belief in our future today than ever before.

Once you see that everything in your past had its time, it's easier to trust that the same will be true for your future. It's because of this that currently rather than worrying about what's ahead, I can feel excitement instead. I don't have to worry about every decision either. God used, and uses, every single step in our journey to work towards His greater plan. For that reason, I'm not sure there's such a thing as a bad or wrong decision after all.

## #5: You are bigger than your fears and failures!

All my life I would have considered myself a confident person. I gained confidence through a variety of achievements. I did well in school, earned a master's degree, landed a good job, found a great person to marry, etc. What I realized along my detour, though, was that deep down, I wasn't truly confident. I only believed in myself through the things I felt comfortable doing. My confidence fully depended on what I had already achieved or on things that came naturally.

When everything comfortable in my life—my plans, my teaching job, my family, a stationary life in the suburbs—was gone, I had zero confidence left. Everything at that point was out of my comfort zone. I didn't gain my true, deep-rooted confidence until I pushed past that comfort zone and overcame the fears and challenges that were surrounding me (quitting teaching, losing my identity, opening up through writing, learning new skills, skydiving, etc.).

Following a detour into the unknown is downright uncomfortable, and you'll feel extremely vulnerable. Your fears are going to be louder than ever; therefore, you have to gain the confidence to be bigger than those fears. You must believe that you are capable and deserving of anything. Regardless of your past or what you have to overcome, anything can be yours! You might not believe in yourself right away, like me, and that's okay. The first step to believing in yourself is being willing to step into the unknown. You have to face those fears head-on, with or without confidence. In fact, one of my favorite quotes is "If your dreams don't scare you, you're doing something wrong." That fear is actually a sign that you're on the right path and headed for greatness.

Let's talk about facing those fears. Fear is that negative, mean voice that tries to stop you when you're about to do something awesome:

- "You're not good-smart-strong-brave enough."
- "You're a failure and you can't do this!"
- "You don't deserve it!"
- "This isn't going to work. You're going to end up worse off."

Pay attention to what your fears are telling you. It may feel counterintuitive to listen to fear's messages, but you can't fight back at your fears if you don't acknowledge them. Identifying your fear gives you the opportunity to take away its powerful hold on you by replacing it with a truth. If you can't find a positive and empowering truth to replace it with, here are some from the Bible for you:

- Romans 5:8: "You are loved, just as you are."
- Ephesians 2:10: "You are God's work of art."
- 1 John 1:9: "You are forgiven."
- 1 John 3:1–2: "You are a child of God."
- 1 Corinthians 3:16 "You are God's temple and His spirit dwells in you."
- Romans 8:31: "God is for you, not against you."

The more you face your fears, the more opportunities you have to learn to believe in yourself. I eventually learned that fears are nothing more than lies or self-doubt. They stem from a variety of things, but fears are very rarely, if ever, accurate.

I know this because fears are limiting, hurtful, deceiving, and bad. I also know that God is good, and nothing that is not good can come from God. God is love, truth, and light. You can rest assured that those fearful thoughts and feelings are not from Him. They are, therefore, not true.

The biggest fear we all face is the fear of failure. We may not have a lot of confidence in ourselves, but we sure do have a lot of pride. We hold on tight to that pride. The thought of losing it and embarrassing ourselves is all it takes for us to shut down and not take action.

The fear of failure comes from worrying what other people will think of us. We worry how others will judge every decision we make, action we take, and outcome we get. Think about it—you're much more willing to embarrass yourself when you're alone. When you're behind closed doors and have nobody there to judge you. So, I can tell you all the typical things you already know about failure. I can tell you things like: "You only fail if you don't try" and "Failure is the key to success." But, we should go straight to the source, which brings us to the next principle in the detour mindset.

## #6: Everyone has their own unique journey.

A major mindset killer, we've discovered, is comparison. It feels impossible *not* to compare your life to others', especially with social media. But, you have to try to avoid it at all costs. The problem is, you only compare your shortcomings to their blessings or advantages. But, do you ever take the time to evaluate if your short comings are truly negative? Do you take *your* advantages into account? Let me give you an example.

Sometimes I'll compare myself to women in my life who have beautiful little families. They love being mamas and have what seems like a picture-perfect life. It's easy to get jealous that they have something I don't have. But, instead, I'll find things about my life that they might be jealous of me for. The truth is, everyone has sacrifices they are making for the life they are living.

Here are things I remind myself when comparison gets the best of me: I love my husband and our marriage. We get so much quality time together and have built a strong foundation for a lifetime together. Many couples with kids have told us they miss that one-on-one time together and wish they would've done more traveling before having kids.

I also love our lifestyle full of freedom and flexibility. I'm grateful for all the places we've traveled and the experiences we've gained. I also get uninterrupted sleep every night. My schedule and activities aren't dictated around kids' lives. Plus, I can live and make decisions somewhat selfishly because I don't have other lives depending on me.

It goes back to having gratitude. I can choose to focus on what I don't have or on what I do have. Sure, I wish I had little humans who showed me the deepest meaning of love every day. I wish I could tuck them in bed at night and read them bedtime stories and give them kisses. I wish I could teach them about the world and inspire them to do big things in it. Maybe someday I'll get that, or maybe I won't. But that won't determine my purpose, happiness, or whether I'm fulfilled or not.

The bottom line is, there's a tradeoff for many things in life. As much as I may want to be a mom, I would never trade being one for the past few years I've experienced. Just as all the moms out there would never trade their children for my life. We all have to do our best with the hand we've been dealt. We're all on our own unique journeys.

Try to find peace in every season of life and remember that God's timing and plan is not only perfect, but it's perfect for YOU. Trust that if something wasn't given to you, it wasn't meant to be yours for reasons that someday you'll know. Nobody "has it all," *nobody*! Everybody is fighting their own battles and insecurities. Everyone is comparing their life to someone else's too. We're all in this thing called life together. We have to have faith in our *own* journeys. It's not a race or a competition.

## #7: Seek change and opportunities to take risks.

When you have a detour mindset, you learn to love change. Change no longer scares you, and you'll find yourself seeking out detours on detours on detours! If it's scary, you run towards it! Risky? You jump feet first. Fear? It's got nothing on you! Sound extreme? It kind of is, and if you don't believe you'll ever get there, stay with me anyway.

Following a detour will show you the possibility of a future better than you could've pictured in your wildest dreams. It changes you big time! As I've shared, once you take that initial scary step onto your new path, you realize how easy it is to go for it. You gain confidence as you explore the unknown. You'll find yourself in situations that require more and more courage. Soon enough, you'll feel the powerful beast inside you coming out.

You'll learn that growth comes from those times you feel uncomfortable. Your strength comes from overcoming the times you're filled with fear and uncertainty, or the times when you feel alone because no one quite understands you. The growth becomes addicting! You'll start to associate uncomfortable moments with feelings of achievement and satisfaction. Naturally, you'll want more!

Does that exhilarate you or terrify you? Or both? I'm actually feeling both of those emotions right now as I sit and write this book. Five years ago, back when I was teaching, if someone would have told me I'd be where I am today, I would have never believed them. But, detours, I tell you . . . they do something crazy to you. So, consider this your warning because you're on your way.

## It Takes Practice

Adopting the detour mindset is the perfect way to start preparing yourself for the greater plans that will unfold along your journey. But, it takes more than choosing to have it. It's a mindset you'll have to work at every single day. It won't come naturally.

Dan and I have found that it can be hard work at times. It starts with simply understanding and believing that it's a crucial part of finding your happiness. Then, it's about daily practice and establishing new habits.

As you start to go after your dreams and take the risks necessary to get there, you'll have to think about who you need to become to be ready for those dreams. You have a lot of work to do with yourself in order to appreciate what God has planned for you. Think about who you want to be and where you want to go. How can you start preparing? It's time to become the best version of yourself.

Because negativity tries to hijack everybody's minds immediately upon waking, Dan and I spend time each morning getting our mindset right for the day. Here's what we do to ground ourselves in a detour mindset throughout the day:

*Journaling*—during my morning journaling, I start by reading the Bible. I try to hear any messages that God wants me to hear for the day and write them down. Sometimes I don't hear anything, but every time I learn more about His character and His love for me. Filling my mind and heart with His word is like putting on armor to protect myself from harmful thoughts and feelings throughout the day.

Journaling looks different for me almost daily. Sometimes it's all prayer, sometimes it's affirmations or writing out my intentions for the day. Other times, I don't write anything, but I read what I've written in the past and appreciate how much I've grown. You start to learn what you need, and the nice thing is, there are no rules with journaling. If you're new to journaling, you can find tons of guides out there. A guide will prompt you in your writing and help you explore the many possibilities for developing a journaling practice.

*Gratitude*—I write down what I'm grateful for in my journal or list it out in my prayers. Other times I'll casually share what I'm grateful for with Dan while walking the dogs or lying in bed at night. It doesn't matter where or how I do it, but every day I take the time to list all the things I'm grateful for that day. I try to be specific, even if it's something seemingly small. You can be grateful for your cup of coffee, a pay raise, a clean house, or healing from an illness . . . everything counts! Even if it feels forced at first, you'll eventually begin to feel it deep down. As a result, thoughts about your shortcomings seem to disappear. It's important to practice gratitude daily. We are humans, and no matter what, we go back to our selfish ways pretty quickly! Daily gratitude practice helps keep this tendency in good check!

*Meditation*—I'm still learning this one and will be the first to tell you it's something you have to practice a lot. Again, it will feel forced for awhile. But, I've come to love it. It's like giving my mind a little nap (and if I'm lucky, I'll sneak one in for my body too!). You only need five minutes of daily meditation, but I'm finding myself wanting twenty now that I am learning how to relax into it. There are lots of guided meditations to help you get started.

What I love about meditating is that it can be a huge source of defense against the negativity in your thoughts. Once you learn how to meditate, you'll catch yourself doing it throughout your day, in tiny bits. You'll breathe through your stress and tension, relax your body, and instantly feel so much better!

*Exercise*—I've always known that exercise boosts your mood. I've heard the science behind it, and everyone who has ever exercised knows how great you feel afterwards. I don't know about you, though, but that has rarely been enough motivation for me to hit the gym. My excuses are far too powerful; that is, until I started noticing that the stronger my body feels, the stronger my mind feels. Getting through a tough workout can feel similar to getting through a tough season in life. You want to give up but know you can't. You keep pushing through it even though it hurts. Best of all, you feel like a million bucks when you finish, and it's one of the greatest accomplishments of your day and a huge confidence booster!

## A Mindset to Believe In

A detour mindset will help you navigate life's seeming dead ends and the unexpected turns along your journey. It will also help you stop worrying about having a perfectly planned-out route. It'll give you the peace in knowing you can handle anything that stops you in your tracks. This mindset will allow you to stop wishing for a map and stop rushing towards a destination. Instead, you'll take your time and enjoy every part along your journey.

My hope for you is that when you come to a dead end in life, despite how much it hurts, you believe something good will come of it. When you come to those detours, I hope you follow them knowing that someday, it will make sense. It's likely that it's not a dead end at all, but actually the beginning of a new journey and a new chapter of your unique story.

You may not know it yet, but you're going to have an incredible story to tell someday. You may not yet understand it, but later you'll be so thankful for the pain you may be feeling right now. And you may not believe it now, but this "dead end" will shape you into the greatest and truest you there ever was. As long as you're willing to follow your detour.

# You're Invited!

## I'd love to connect with you!

I shared my story, now it's your turn. Please write me and share your story with me—your dead ends, your detours, your achievements, and everything in between! I'd genuinely love to hear from you, learn from you, and support you. Here's how you can contact me:

    Email — lindsay@followyourdetour.com
    Facebook — @followyourdetour
    Instagram — @follow_your_detour

I'd also love it if you checked out our blog, FollowYourDetour.com. You can read about and see photos of our adventures and the various experiences I wrote about in this book. If you'd like to receive updates, be sure to subscribe to our email list

# Can You Help?

## Thank You for Reading My Book!

I'd really appreciate your feedback and would love to hear what you have to say. Your input will be valuable in making my future books better. Please leave me an honest review on Amazon letting me know what you thought of the book.

Thanks so much!

Lindsay

# Acknowledgments

Following our detour would have never been possible without the unconditional love and support of our entire family. Thank you for always encouraging us and never questioning all our crazy adventures. Thank you for continually urging us to go and find our happiness even though it hurts for us to be away. I thank God every single day for blessing me with the greatest family imaginable. Especially all my nieces and nephews who I love as if they were my own and who help fill that desire of my heart!

Throughout my life, I've also been touched by so many wonderful friends, who I consider to be more like "angels". I hope you all know who you are and the impact you've had on me and especially my detour. I'm continually blown away by the incredible support network I have in you all. I truly can't say thank you enough!

Writing this book has been a huge labor of love. I am so grateful for all the people who had a part in helping me accomplish this dream of mine. Thank you to my husband who is my rock, my SPS coach Gary for his guidance, my kind and talented editor Nancy, and my awesome launch team! I couldn't have done it without you all!

Lastly, thank you to every person who has been following our detour through our blog and social media. While we've never met many of you, you have so kindly supported us through your encouraging emails, messages, and comments. We read every one, and they mean the world to us.

# About the Author

Lindsay McKenzie is a writer, adventurer, and the co-founder of Follow Your Detour. Lindsay dedicated six years to teaching kindergarten before embarking on a new life adventure: full-time RVing. She is now a top travel-and-lifestyle blogger, inspiring thousands of readers every day with her heartfelt writing and storytelling.

Originally from Colorado, Lindsay travels with her husband and two dogs. They are currently exploring the US while living in their Winnebago. You can follow their adventures and enjoy their travel photos and advice at FollowYourDetour.com and on their social media channels. Lindsay loves connecting and building relationships with her readers, and she encourages you to contact her at lindsay@followyourdetour.com.

www.ingramcontent.com/pod-product-compliance
Lightning Source LLC
Chambersburg PA
CBHW020415080526
44584CB00014B/1333